T0277653

MEDICINE WHEEL FOR THE PLANET

MEDICINE WHEEL FOR THE PLANET

A JOURNEY TOWARD PERSONAL AND ECOLOGICAL HEALING

DR. JENNIFER GRENZ

UNIVERSITY OF MINNESOTA PRESS

MINNEAPOLIS

First University of Minnesota Press edition, 2024

Published by arrangement with Knopf Canada/Penguin Random House Canada

Published by the University of Minnesota Press
111 Third Avenue South, Suite 290
Minneapolis, MN 55401-2520
http://www.upress.umn.edu

ISBN 978-1-5179-1646-6 (hc)

A Cataloging-in-Publication record for this book is available from the Library of Congress.

Printed in Canada on acid-free paper

The University of Minnesota is an equal-opportunity educator and employer.

33 32 31 30 29 28 27 26 25 24   10 9 8 7 6 5 4 3 2 1

CONTENTS

My Shelhsteelt (Pivotal Moment): From Ecologist to Land Healer

MY ORIGINAL sense of connection to the land began in my great-grandmother's garden when I was very little. Fleeting memories of eating giant tomatoes like apples and running to get the salt and pepper shakers hanging on the fence to sprinkle between every delicious bite. Or perhaps it began long before that, as caring for plants and growing food may very well be part of my DNA.

My family comes from what is referred to as the Interior, a region of British Columbia (BC), Canada. We are "people of the canyon" with deep histories of movement up and down the Fraser and Thompson Rivers, which meet in Kumsheen, known today as Lytton—the town that made global news in 2021 when wildfire overtook it in a matter of minutes. My Nlaka'pamux great-grandmother and my Secwepemc great-grandfather were very much part of the ranching community in the Shuswap area.

I grew up watching my grandmas, aunties, uncles, and cousins canning just about anything and everything, and I spent many summers fishing on the lakes and rivers within what is, I would learn much later, my traditional territory. My eventual choice in career as an ecologist was a surprise to no one in my family. From early days of following my dad in my rubber boots along the edges of creeks and rivers and through the shrubs that grew over my head, my life's trajectory was set.

With the deafening sound of the river in my ears and the sweet smell of cottonwood in my nose, I remember thinking, at around eight years old, about how deeply I cared for the environment and wondering if that could be a real job. Caring for our lands and waters was "my why." I found out in my first year of university that ecological restoration, work to help with the recovery of ecosystems that have been destroyed or degraded (often because of humans), was indeed a real job. I remember a presentation by a real-life ecologist promoting her line of work in my first-year biology class at the University of Alberta, where I studied before transferring to the University of British Columbia, like it was yesterday. I held my breath as she talked, my heart pounding, so I wouldn't risk missing a word. This is what I was going to do. I've since spent nearly two decades trying to fix and repair ecosystems in coastal BC.

My early interest in ecology and weed science set me on a trajectory for the best work in the world. While serving the health of our planet, I planned and conducted ecological restoration in majestic places alongside equally passionate people. It seemed bigger than all of us, and we felt we could make a real difference in helping our ailing environment. Much of my professional life has been in service to environmental nonprofit organizations where

I had freedom to design, fundraise for, and implement environmental education and outreach campaigns, and to get bodies on the ground to control invasive species and repair the land when they were gone. I have acted as a prominent media spokesperson for invasive species issues, from threats to infrastructure, threats to salmon, and threats to human health, to promotion of solutions, to new possible threats like tsunami debris. I have worked with every level of government, including First Nations. I have had the privilege of working in some of the most sensitive ecosystems in BC. I have stood in front of colleagues, the public, and politicians to rally the troops. Many people—government officials, bureaucrats, volunteers, and concerned citizens—have relied on me for leadership and scientific guidance.

In spite of the many roles I have had within the organizations I've been employed with, I have always seen myself first and foremost as a field practitioner. Someone solving problems in real time in our forests. For me, this meant finding the best way to prevent, control, and contain invasive plant species that threaten the health of the environment, people, and sometimes the economy. I prided myself on the quality of the science I used to inform this work and the science I generated through it.

Meanwhile, I quietly practised traditional medicine at home. As a Nlaka'pamux woman, I lived my other life discreetly. Many of my colleagues were unaware of this "other side": Indigenous me. I nurtured and collected plants I learned about from my Elders and other knowledge keepers to make medicines for my family and friends and for those seeking remedies outside of conventional medicine. I created a comfortable cognitive dissonance that allowed me to engage in traditional knowledge and cultural practices while maintaining my credibility as a woman of science. I'm not even sure I did that on purpose. In fact, I know I didn't. Looking back, I can see that it had become as natural as a tree bending to the wind. I had seen what happened to those who attempted to present alternative ecological perspectives to my colleagues. I had even joined in on the eye rolls and jokes about those who did.

Self-protection is a funny thing.

This state of dissonance led to an ultra-slow-motion professional unravelling. While the environmental restoration work we did was often rewarding—some of it did help—there were many projects that failed. A collection of projects, undertaken alongside an army of other environmental do-gooders, became an exercise in futility.

I battled my way through the prickles. Thorns scraping my arms, catching the sleeves of my jacket and my pant legs, poking through my gloves. It seemed an unattainable goal, bringing this wall of Himalayan blackberry down, cane by cane. But there we were. On a mission greater than ourselves. Clear the wall of the invader so we could plant native plants in its place. Innumerable Saturdays spent leading these armies in terrible weather, arms bleeding. If we made it through the thorny thicket, we dragged heavy pots of lovingly grown native plants across the park, dug holes while talking about our plans for the rest of the weekend, sometimes talking about our despair over the state of the watershed, plugged these green saviours into the ground, and high-fived each other, victorious as we carried our shovels back to our cars. Soaking wet. Warmed by the goodness of the work.

It seems naive now.

For all those Saturdays, I struggle to think of a single site where the flag of our environmental victory remains planted. Pardon the pun. Instead of the fulfillment of my vision of a flourishing native plant community as a memorial for the battle against invasive plants that once took place there, upon returning to the site only twelve weeks later, I found myself staring at a tangled mess of the invader's canes once more. The green saviours seemingly vanished . . .

Repeat. Repeat. Repeat.

One site in particular can be credited with the onset of my chronic case of "environmental do-gooder angst." A condition best described as an overwhelming heap of self-doubt leading an environmental steward to question all they had ever learned or done and what their future was in all of it. Suddenly, altruism wasn't enough of an antidote to persevere.

I was leading a group of at-risk youth planting conifers across what was an old landfill. Funding provided by an organization looking to plant trees to reduce CO_2. A noble but misguided mission of Western science. The weather was horrible. The site worse. Shovelling in muck, dragging potted trees weighing fifty pounds or more up hills for long distances, with kids looking to improve their lives. I tried to set a positive example and the kids nicknamed me "Hardcore," which gave me hope that if this environmentalist thing didn't pan out, I may have a future in acting. The project took two months. My muscles burned; my fingers and toes were often numb with cold. As I dragged and shovelled, my inner voice asked questions that went beyond my usual professional skepticism. Why are we doing this? Does this make sense? Are these the right trees? Is this the right medium for planting? What is the point of this? What is this site supposed to be? What happens after this? Who is going to care for these trees when it gets hot across this vast, shadeless landscape? What about forest succession?

After the project was finished, hundreds of conifers were planted in a Christmas tree–lot fashion. I remember thinking how incredibly weird and disconnected the whole venture seemed. We praised the youth for their environmental victory, and I never gave voice to my inner doubt.

There is an unspoken agreement in my line of work not to articulate the feelings behind the knowing glances shared with colleagues. Two years later, one of those youth came back to visit me. They told me that they had seen the site from the road and it looked like every single tree was dead. A friend confirmed it. Every. Single. Tree. Was. Dead. I couldn't go back to see it for myself.

Over time I began vocalizing my concerns on these matters, only to realize that they weren't well received by my colleagues. I wrestled with questions like: What was it that kept us going through these failures? What was it about the work that made it seem right? And what was it that also seemed so wrong? What were we missing that we just couldn't seem to win? What did it mean to win?

After ten years of this mind wrestling, my work no longer felt good, and sometimes it even felt pointless. Then sometimes became most times. It was an indescribable personal crisis, one that thrust me into turning my life upside down in hopes of finding my ecological mojo once more. Maybe graduate school would help. A break from the front lines of environmental work that can be depressingly difficult and seemingly futile. A break from the front lines of planet-saving to think about how it could all be done differently. Our ecosystems clearly needed more wins.

It was at the beginning of my graduate school journey, during this period of deep reflection and self-doubt, uncertain of my path forward, that I met Luschiim for the first time. Luschiim, also known as Dr. Arvid Charlie, is an Elder and important knowledge holder of the Quw'utsun (Cowichan) People, whose traditional territory stretches from the middle east coast of Vancouver Island across the waters of the Salish Sea to the coastal mainland of BC along portions of the south arm of the Fraser River. His knowledge connects us to that of his grandfather who lived over one hundred years ago. I was one of a group of graduate students working on the restoration of Cowichan Tribes' ancient village site, Ye'yumnuts, which was the place and focus of my PhD research. It is a rare gift to hear someone speak of our (Indigenous Peoples') relationship with the land before settlers, and to hear first-hand the resilience of someone who has lived through colonial policies and structures that continue today. Luschiim represents a connection to a time when we cared for the land our way, and he carries the wisdom of how we can once again connect with and heal the land, our way.

Looking back now, I can see that I clung desperately to each of Luschiim's words as he spoke what was in my heart. His words provided me with a lifeline to fulfilling who I was meant to be: not simply a Western-trained scientist, but an Indigenous woman in restoration ecology, bringing healing to our lands our way. It was as if Luschiim, seeing the distress behind my eyes, came over and placed my hand upon this woven line and nodded decisively in the direction it gently pulled me toward; the direction I wanted to go but was too scared to. Sometimes you just need an Elder to usher you along.

It is important to understand that colonization is not a single event in the past, but a continuous process that carries on today; one that has brought and continues to bring devastation to both our people and the environment. A perpetuation of the settler worldview rooted in Judeo-Christian belief that gives people dominion over the other creatures of the Earth and objectifies what is referred to as "the environment" as if it is independent from humans. Foundational ideas established by settlers that have resulted in policies and actions that continue to attempt to separate us from our land.

Our Indigenous worldview does not allow for such separation. Our very existence is inside the ecosystem as an equal relation, meaning we are just as important as the grasshoppers, worms, birds, and soils are. Yet we find ourselves living in a world hampered by colonial legacies that continue to force us outside the ecosystem. A reality that compromises our cultural identity and very existence in the world. We watch as the settlers tinker with elements of "nature" in hopes of repairing the harm they have caused. We watch them trying to fix things from the outside of the ecosystem, a vantage point that divides them from our relations on the Earth—the very relations they are trying to help. A vantage point that is difficult to understand for an Indigenous person such as myself, and that is clearly not leading us toward the level of ecological reconciliation we need now.

While the world wakes up to the true history of Turtle Island—genocide, forced assimilation, residential schools, stolen lands and waters, and stolen children—we cannot neglect to acknowledge the continued influence of Christian ideologies today. They remain the cornerstone of Western science that disregards and denigrates Indigenous knowledges. They perpetuate the pursuit of a return to Eden as the goal of restoration ecology.

The colonial rulers of Turtle Island may have thought they succeeded in separating us from our lands and worldviews, as we seemingly embraced their agrarian practices, engaged in their commerce, and yielded as they barred us from engaging in traditional practices. While we may have adapted to the world they thrust upon us, they do not know what we have continued to carry in our hearts. Our ancestral knowledges and our connection with our lands and waters have never left us. We have been an adaptive and resilient people in waiting and our time is now.

During our initial meeting with Luschiim, he asked the graduate students what brought us to our research. I shared this story of the moment in my career that made me realize I just couldn't keep working as I had anymore.

I had been sent with the Watchmen of an Indigenous community to survey and control an isolated infestation of an invasive plant species along a river on the community's land. Called Early Detection Rapid Response, it was an opportunity to protect the river and its native flora and fauna from the spread of this species while its populations were still small.

Once we arrived at the site, I went to grab my equipment, ready to take on the interlopers with gratifying zeal. An Elder grabbed my arm. "Let's just go look at the plants first," he said. Perplexed, but never one to disrespect an Elder, I followed him and the other Watchmen to the site. He sat down and motioned for me to sit beside him. I sat and began to share my thoughts about what we should do. He put his finger to his lips to shush me and pointed at the plants. So, we sat and stared at the plants.

At first it felt like an eternity, a confusing waste of time. And then, I could see the plants, the surrounding trees, the limits of the infestation, the small breaks in the tree canopy, the position of the sun relative to them, the skeletal structure of leaves eaten by slugs, and I noticed the small size of the plants relative to their cousins living in other locations at that time of year. Then we sat some more. Finally, he stood and offered me a hand up. We quietly walked to our quads and drove away from the site.

I visit this site almost every year. Some years there have been none of the invasive plants. Other years, a couple of small ones, but never the explosion of invasive plants I almost used to hope would appear so that my world could make sense again. A world of predictability in the science I knew. A simplicity in seeing the world in one way instead of in relation with everything else.

After I shared my story, Luschiim told me, "That is your shelhstamut." *Shelhstamut* is a word in Hul'q'umi'num', the language of the Cowichan People, meaning "a new path for you" created in a pivotal moment. My shelhsteelt ("a new path for me") launched me on this journey into graduate studies and triggered a realization that there was no way I could go back to working as I had as a field practitioner in restoration ecology. While I worried about facing ridicule and resistance to change among my colleagues, I knew I had to find a new path that would give me the freedom to work in a way that was congruent with who I am: an Indigenous ecologist. Even if that meant challenging and questioning the tenets of the field. Grad school would be the place for that—a place to start again. In a good way. Whatever that meant.

Some of my friends and family thought I was making the wrong decision. Why would I throw away a successful career? It was difficult to explain the pain I felt in a job that looked to outsiders like I was making a real impact helping our environment. The pain I felt at my core was a mixture of ecological grief from our failures—continued invasion of invasive species, dead trees and native plants we painstakingly planted, collapsing salmon populations—and the weight of working from a worldview that was both not mine, and not as effective as our planet needed. It was time to stop taking the same approaches and hoping for different results. From that moment in that room with Luschiim, I knew I'd made the right choice. This was the path to something different. Though I still did not understand exactly what the journey ahead of me was or even what the destination would look like, I was free of the burden of questioning or even rationalizing my decision. It felt like a new direction yet directionless at the same time. The fact was, it didn't matter what that path would lead to, it was the right path to take. I found balm in something much later in the journey that Elder Peter Williams, also from Cowichan Tribes, said to me. He said, "The greatest distance a man must travel is between his head and his heart."

This book is about the journey to connect my head (Western science) and my heart (my Indigenous worldview). A journey of both personal and ecological reconciliation. What led me to my shelhsteelt were many moments of hesitation, of uncertainty, of discomfort throughout my professional life. I see them now as ancestral taps on the shoulder, warning of the colonial influences that affected how we related with our ecosystem and all our relations within it. Ancestral taps meant to remind me that I was indeed an Indigenous woman, first. Taps that expressed frustration that we needed only to look to our ancestors to understand why we weren't making enough of a difference even with the efforts of many great people and minds. I had learned to ignore those taps in the name of good science—in fact, I was taught to ignore them. The tapping over time had become more and more incessant, overwhelming, and impossible to disregard. I learned to listen to and embrace it.

As it seemingly rang in my ears during my shelhsteelt, it was undeniable that it was time for me to go back and get to know my ancestors, to reclaim my culture, and to listen to the knowledge keepers here today. I had to do the work to heal myself so I could help our planet in the best way possible. Suddenly I understood what "we are the land" meant. All I'd ever wanted to do was to bring healing to our lands and waters; however, I hadn't realized it would require me to accomplish something so personal: connecting heart and head. Perhaps that was the first and most important lesson of this journey.

Facing more than a decade of professional work with new eyes is unsettling. What would the lens of the Indigenous worldview reveal? The possibility of undermining myself seemed both terrifying and freeing. I knew that it would be hard to look at the familiar in an entirely different way. This shift would be more difficult than simply putting on new glasses—it would require a conscious effort to prepare myself to "see" in this new way. A way that should not have been new to me, but the colonized history of my family made it so. Sure, I had fleeting glances through their lenses during my childhood in my great-grandma's garden and during my career when what we were doing didn't seem to make sense, but those relational glasses of my Indigeneity remained so far from my grasp, I didn't realize they were mine to wear. No one told me I could wear them. No one told me how.

Until Luschiim did.

The ancestral shoulder tapping had morphed into the drumbeat that drove forward my journey. A journey to find the answers to questions that had worn upon me for too long, like water on a stone.

What would ancestral wisdom tell us about healing our planet if we listened and allowed ourselves to see beyond the confines of a singular worldview?

My goal as an Indigenous researcher is not simply to do research and report back. True to our Indigenous, relational worldview, my goal as a researcher is to help strengthen your connection to this work through my own story. A story that was not a linear, one-directional path to connect head and heart, but a circular one.

One that followed the path of the medicine wheel, the teachings of each direction necessary to get to the next. These teachings stretched me in profound ways and, once completed, gave me the power to move freely between head and heart to see the land and her people and science anew. A power necessary to heal the planet.

As I continue to expand my personal network of Indigenous Peoples working in academia across the world, I have noticed that our relational worldview, focused on the interconnectedness of all relations and our land, is what unites us. It is important, however, to acknowledge that the work I present here is certainly limited by its regionality. It is a common mistake to assume that all Indigenous communities think the same way and have the same opinions. It is that mistake that leads to the tokenism of Indigenous Peoples. Indigenous communities are different. We come from different Nations and thus our histories, stories, and cultures are different. Our lands and waters are different. Within Indigenous communities you are likely to find a spectrum of opinions on a myriad of topics, just like any other community. The work I did was largely completed with Cowichan Tribes with the influence of Coast Salish and Kwakwaka'wakw knowledge holders and my own Nlaka'pamux teachings; it is most certainly not representative of all Indigenous Peoples. I might have come to different conclusions had my research journey taken place largely on other lands.

I hope as we experience this journey together that you may also see yourself in it so that it will have power in your own life. That as you read, you understand what is behind this quest to decolonize and Indigenize ecological restoration so that we can heal the land together. So come with me around the medicine wheel as I cannot do this work alone.

Part One

A
Spark
in the
North

WE BEGIN our journey with the teachings of the northern direction of the medicine wheel. The North, where the snow, the colour white, reminds us of the hair of our Elders. The place we draw not only upon their knowledges but, most importantly, upon their wisdom. A wisdom missing from modern ecology. A wisdom that is the spark from which the fire beneath me is lit to do better for our planet.

I.

The Power of Stories

Stories. To teach us. To guide us. To connect us.
To all beings. To the past. To the now. To the future.
They are alive.

STORIES ARE a sacred and integral part of our Indigenous way of life. They provide a way for us to understand our place in the world. Our stories can be as grand as an explanation of our origins involving the animal and spirit worlds, or—no less profound—as simple as the sharing of a personal experience. Our stories are meant to be dynamic in nature, every storyteller making changes to meet the needs of the listener and as an acknowledgement of the ever-changing tides of our world. Our stories are as diverse as the beautiful Indigenous Peoples across our Earth Mother, and their differences are celebrated, admired, and respected. While Indigenous stories may differ in content and context, they are united in the power of their telling as ceremonies that connect us to important lessons. Stories are received as treasured gifts to be held in our hearts, and the recipient has a responsibility to share them with those who may need them.

I have received such treasured gifts and accept the responsibility to share them with those who are interested in living a life with the purpose of healing our sick Earth Mother. At a time where we face the uncertainty of a rapidly changing climate and when, despite many of our best efforts, we are not making the difference we need to, these stories form a new foundation from which we heal the land. These stories, if we listen, are the spark that can change ecology.

Stories as tools of learning are as valid as the findings of research conducted using the Western scientific method. Stories are data. I realize that can be difficult to accept. It was for me at first, but once I opened myself up to the stories as science, I realized that Western science and Indigenous knowledges are not diametrically opposed knowledge systems. While they are often described as different "ways of knowing," this descriptor can be misleading and may contribute to some of the resistance expressed by members of the dominant, Western scientific community. I think that very often we are trying to know similar things; we just may be seeking that knowledge differently.

The phrase "ways of knowing" continues to assert a colonial narrative upon Indigenous Peoples, perpetuating a commonly held perception that our knowledges are—that *we* are—limited to the past, while in fact, we are here today. It suggests that our knowledges are only a recounting of our pre-contact history, and that we only use our Indigenous "ways of knowing" to inform us, which supports the false idea that we are looking to replace, denigrate, or entirely disregard Western science. I see these knowledge systems, Indigenous knowledge and Western science, not as different "ways of knowing," but rather as different "ways of understanding." Both have so much to offer because of their differences. Both are generative in the modern context. Each can act as a catalyst for the other. Together, they provide a more accessible and complete picture. Sometimes we need more of one than the other. That's it. Neither is better. They are simply better together. Both are science.

There are branches of science that could benefit greatly from the application of different "ways of understanding." Ecology is such an example. Simply defined, ecology is a branch of science concerned with the interrelationship of organisms and their environments. What better way to study relationships than to focus on the stories of those relationships? For example, instead of limiting our focus to the mechanisms of how organisms function in relation to one another, we might ask, How do they know each other? Where do we find them together? Where don't we? How long has this relationship been noticed? It seems this more personal line of questioning should be inherently a part of this field of study. Unfortunately, this way of understanding has not had the opportunity to influence this complicated field of study in a way that realizes its full potential. Storytelling is no stranger to ecology; in fact, it has had an impact on modern ecology, just not in the way that it should.

Learning about the world and our place within it through stories is not unique to Indigenous Peoples. Ecology finds itself atop a foundational story surprising to many working within it: Christianity. The origin story of humans upon our planet, told by the dominant religion practised by European settlers in North

America, has had significant consequences for our relationship with the Earth. This observation is not new and is certainly not meant to be a criticism of the Christian faith. It is meant to draw attention to the depth of the colonial influences upon our land that not only harm it but may be inhibiting the effectiveness of our efforts to heal Her today. This foundational story limits other stories from broadening our understanding of the complex nature of the many relationships upon our Earth. The dominance of this origin story is difficult if not impossible to overcome. This is why the spark presented by Indigenous ways of understanding—those rooted in the relational nature of storytelling—should motivate a shift to a different foundation for ecology. One that makes room for more types of storytelling from the myriad of Indigenous knowledges around the world. One that makes ecological reconciliation possible.

Modern ecology is rooted in the narrative of the perfect creation of Earth by God who later added His perfect human creations, Adam and Eve, in the image of Himself. They resided within the Garden of Eden with the intention to multiply, to steward over the Earth, all in complete obedience to God . . . until that fateful day. Their fall from grace was the impetus for the lifelong human quest of restoration and a return to Eden.

While that was a very simple summary, this story and its influence in the shaping of Western society have laid the groundwork for what I refer to as Eden ecology. An ecology with notions of perfectionism of the environment. An ecology where perfection was broken by the introduction of humans as they fell from grace, and humans are blamed for the resulting imbalance of the once-perfect world. Where the ultimate goal is to restore, to put things back the way they were when they were perfect. This return-to-Eden narrative resonates through the terminology, research, and goals of restoration ecology. It has given rise to an ecology based on dichotomies, hierarchies, and notions of perfectionism. All of which are hindering our progress in healing the land at this critical juncture of our climate history.

The absolute nature of a religion based on righteousness and dogma, rooted in a written tradition, often places it at odds with Indigenous belief systems, values, and knowledges. While it is difficult in the context of Western science to entertain discussions about spirituality and knowledges passed through oral tradition, it is critical to understanding both the failings of modern restoration ecology and the potential contributions of Indigenous ways of understanding to address those failings. In a famous 1854 speech, Chief Seattle said:

> Your religion was written upon tablets of stone by the iron finger of your God so that you could never forget. The Red Man could never comprehend or remember it. Our religion is the traditions of our ancestors—the dreams of our old men, given to them in solemn hours of the night by the Great Spirit; and the visions of our sachems, and is written in the hearts of our people.

I do not think the influence of the story of the Garden of Eden on ecology was purposeful. Ecology as a field of study developed in the aftermath of the colonial tsunami meant to wipe out the Indigenous people and their collective memory of an ecology lived since time immemorial. Since its emergence, ecology has been on its own journey, moving with the colonial current. While its journey is not without academic debate and controversy, it has not resisted its foundational story. Even as ecology shifts today to include Indigenous knowledge, it does so through extractive practices similar to those of early days as our People showed the explorer men, now renowned as the "fathers" of ecology or botany, our plants and their uses to be documented and renamed. Just as we were documented by Indian agents and given Christian names.

Today assimilation has become sneakier. Under the guise of inclusion, the remaining threads of our collective memories, of stewarding our lands and waters our way, are taken from us and woven into the comfortable, colonial way of understanding. The result leaves our threads barely visible.

For a time, invisibility was a goal thrust upon Indigenous Peoples. A tack necessary to survive the colonial tsunami and exist within its aftermath. In the early twentieth century, my great-great-grandfather foresaw what was coming, what registration by Indian agents would bring upon our People. He used the deep ties of our family to the ranching community in the Shuswap region of British Columbia to hide his family and subsequent generations in plain sight. Pretending to be a rancher from Mexico, he fiercely adopted a settler way of life. His son, my great-grandfather, fluent in the Secwepemc language, was raised to deny who he was and never speak of it. As an adult he even referred to his own people as "those dirty Indians," a phrase his children remember he and my great-grandmother using. My grandmother and her siblings were met with stern words and punishment if they ever dared to bring up the question of their identity. Even in the later years of my great-grandfather's life, when it was no longer as unsafe to admit his identity, he refused to have his family live on the reserve, though a house was offered to him.

The multigenerational denial of my family's identity was so successful, we were not Indigenous according to the colonial government's paperwork. This led to a quest over a decade long by my great-uncle William (Bill) Sworts to prove our Indigeneity and bring healing to our family. For a time, I felt angry that this was our family's story. We were the Indigenous kids with no idea about our culture. We only lived the intergenerational trauma without understanding where it came from. My heart has softened, and I felt ashamed of that anger when I became a mother myself. My great-uncle Bill's stories of overhearing his mother crying to his father at night, worried that they would be found out and that their children would be taken, took on a new depth of meaning. Theirs was a reality I can't fathom.

The wisdom and bravery of my great-grandfather and his father are difficult to find words for. They spared a large part of the family tree the trauma of residential school. They kept my grandma and her siblings safe. Great-Grandpa taught them to hide from the Indian agents when they would come in the trucks to the nearby reserve in Clinton to take Native children. My great-auntie Louise described to me how her own friends were taken and never seen again. She recalls the shouting and screaming of children and the crying of their mothers. Assimilation saved us. That is something I still cannot fully process. I raise it here as I know my family is not alone in this experience. It is a story of the legacy of residential schools that often goes untold. Those who survived by divorcing their culture and denying their own relatives. Those who chose invisibility.

———

Stories are so powerful that they take on a life of their own and become embedded in every facet of our being without us even realizing it. The story of denying our family identity continues to attempt to define the successive generations; it has created a profound cognitive dissonance. My own mother describes family vacations to Lillooet to visit her "Native cousins," never realizing that those were her first cousins. Never seeing herself as one of them until she gained Native status as an adult. Her generation were never threatened with punishment for bringing up questions of their identity, because they didn't even know to ask. My mother saw herself like any other white child she grew up with in South Vancouver in the 1950s and 1960s. The story had achieved an unspoken power, obliterating her cultural identity and ancestral ties. To me, the greatest and most insidious power of all.

To reconcile our family identity, my great-uncle Bill spent a painstaking decade taking photographs of headstones in cemeteries and combing through baptismal, birth, marriage, and death records. He went to many museums and historical societies in small towns throughout the Fraser Canyon and Shuswap regions and was able to verify our Indigeneity with the exception of two gaps in our family tree. My great-uncle Bill was unable to "prove" the Indigeneity of his grandmothers, who were not registered by Indian agents, to the Canadian government with the information he had at the time. For example, in a response letter from the government of Canada, they claimed that because there was no baptismal record for his grandmother, Hattie Raines, she could not be Indigenous—a mind-boggling, colonial metric of Indigeneity. It didn't matter that Uncle Bill knew her and had pictures of her indicating she is clearly an

Indigenous woman. He similarly could not prove the Indigenous identity of his other grandmother, referred to in available records at the time only as "Josephine Indian" (no last name), according to the requirements of the colonial paper trail.

Uncle Bill eventually gave up on his battle over the identity of his grandmothers, but he was able to prove the Indigeneity of the rest of the family tree sufficiently enough to get Indian status from the Canadian government. While he felt badly that this status didn't extend to my generation at the time, he felt great relief to finally be recognized (mostly) for who he was. Changes to Canada's Indian Act in 2019 remedied the extension of status for my generation and the next (my children). He told me recently, "Boy, my parents would be rolling in their graves over this." They had worked so hard to hide in plain sight and here we were, trying to unravel the legacy they felt to be their most important achievement. All the records he painstakingly gathered over that decade of identity reclamation, he passed on to me in the spring of 2022. He said, "It's your turn now to finish fixing this."

I took this assignment on in honour of him and our lineages. With the help of a genealogist, in only two days with the modern search tools available, we confirmed the identities of his two grandmothers (my great-great-grandmothers).

It is difficult to take stories back, even when we know they aren't true anymore. The fact is, my family's identity story was true for a long time, and much had been built upon this foundation. Even though my mother is a "Status Indian" according to the government of Canada, when she talks about her Indigeneity she says, "I am not a real Indian." My mother recently lost a friendship that spanned four decades when she was able to get her COVID-19 vaccine ahead of the general population, as Indigenous

Elders were being offered theirs first. It wasn't until one of her best friends cast a slur about "bloody Natives getting their vaccines first" that my mother recognized the racism and felt it personally. This, along with other experiences she had faced previously, hit her hard and all at once. She had encountered racism in the past but didn't recognize it for what it was. Even when my father's father called her "squaw," she didn't process it, attributing to it some other justification.

Some of my mother's younger siblings and cousins have been able to learn about and reclaim our family history and culture. I am so proud to watch my uncle Gary Robinson fulfilling his role as an Elder in the Indigenous communities he works with. My cousins are hunting and fishing on our traditional territory. My generation is working to serve Indigenous communities where we live in various ways—as educational assistants, in health care, and in economic development. While most of us do not live in our traditional territory, we are finding community, and our own children know who they are. We still push back against the power of that foundational family identity story. While it has taken so much from us, we are not just weakening its power, we are writing a new family story.

I found a strange sense of familiarity as I began the journey of re-storying our attempts to heal our planet from the clutches of an Eden ecology. I had felt this sense of urgency and inner conflict before. I had felt driven by a similar need for truth. I knew this same overwhelming drive to overcome the status quo. Upon sharing this with a knowledge keeper friend of mine, he said, "You are living parallel stories of overcoming assimilation." There it was. He was exactly right. This was not an accident—it was the workings and care of the ancestors.

The night after my pivotal conversation with Luschiim, I had a dream. In it, I walked out onto the back deck of our home in twilight to see what seemed like one hundred white owls sitting closely together on the ground on the small hill at the side of our farm. I was frightened at first, wondering if this was a strong sign of death; but as I looked at them all gathered together, I realized they were my ancestors and they had come with a message. They did not speak at first, but all at once I understood. Their message was that they knew I was scared and uncertain, but they were there to remind me that I was already walking this journey around the medicine wheel. Then I heard, "So, walk. Your family is in one hand and our lands in the other. Walk tall and with purpose. Together you will end up where you all need to go."

These assurances seemed to come along exactly when I needed them. I was not only uncertain about what the journey ahead would reveal, but I carried tremendous guilt for questioning the work I had directed and done alongside other well-meaning people for so long. I realized that what was important was the spirit behind why I needed to do this. It was not to dishonour the land; it was an act of love for it. There was purpose behind all of those experiences, I was only returning to them, as I was ready to learn their lessons.

We were heading up the inlet in a boat toward my very favourite workplace. It was the late spring freshet, so the waterfalls were going to be spectacular. I loved their roar in my ears as I worked. The sound drowned out even the sound of my inner voice. It was just me and the plants that way. Still within reach of the disturbance of urban living, we were far enough away that the forest was mostly what we consider "intact" or "healthy." The community of plants was how it was supposed to be, and free of the invasive species. *We were sent here because one invader was beginning to make a comfortable home along the trail from the dock to the waterfalls, leaking into the understorey of alder and cottonwood trees.*

We didn't often try to eradicate Himalayan blackberry in the city. It would be impossible as it is everywhere, growing in the oddest of places and thriving. A free source of food, it is often left as is. In this case, it had overtaken the plant species we would expect to find in the forest understorey. The area was so close to sensitive habitat, where the ecosystem was healthy, that we didn't want it to expand its range farther, its seeds spread by birds. We sprayed the blackberry plants with herbicide in some areas and dug up their roots and cut back their canes in others. As we rode away in the boat back to the city, I thought about how much I looked forward to seeing the results of our work when we would return in the fall. Things put back the way they were supposed to be. Killing weeds can be very gratifying.

When we returned in the fall, after docking the boat I sprinted up the ramp across the path directly into the forest. "What the heck is this?!" I exclaimed as my park ranger friend and field assistant made their way to where I was. We stood in a sea of yellow flowers we had never seen before. "What is this plant?!" I asked again. No one knew. The area was so dense with plants we could barely see the dead canes of the blackberry. I pulled some of the mystery plants to take back with us so we could try to identify them. There are few plants in the region I don't know, so this was both frustrating and perplexing. It was a quiet boat ride back. Hadn't we done what we were supposed to do? We got rid of the invaders. Where was Eden? This may sound naive, but this is how ecological restoration was taught to me. Remove the invasive plants, let the good plants return. After much sleuthing, we learned that the yellow flowering plant from the Impatiens *family was considered a new invader to the region that was just beginning to appear. I couldn't understand how the work we did to kill the blackberry caused a flush of plants to grow that had not been seen before in the area. It made no sense. We did what we were supposed to do and the land didn't do what we expected. A friend said we were "punked" by the forest. Pretty much.*

Ecology over time has pursued an ecological, capital *T* Truth. The Truth of Eden. Truth that has given rise to the modern-day conservation movement. Humans, destroyers of ecosystems, trying to right their wrongs by putting things back the way they're supposed to be. Introduce invasive species, kill them. Cut down trees, plant some more. Hunt animals to extinction, raise and transplant new ones to the area. The human environmental apology tour.

I made a career as a roadie on this tour. At first consideration, it makes sense. We should be fixing what we messed up. The question is, Are we really fixing it or are we working mostly to alleviate our own environmental guilt?

Fresh out of university, I began working for an environmental charity that conducted ecological restoration in the city. I was very excited about being part of something important. The charity got funding from many sources for greening projects. They would gather volunteers together to help at stewardship events. We ordered lots of snacks and drinks, set up our tent, and had volunteers remove invasive plants and then plant the native plants we brought. It was gratifying to see the mountain of invasive plants removed and to see all the newly planted baby plants in their new homes. Stepping back at the end of these events and admiring our work, even when we were in the pouring rain, felt really good. I did more and more of these events, sometimes in settings like public parks and along greenways. Other areas chosen for these activities made me raise an eyebrow, like a random fenceline in an alleyway that was probably only fifteen metres long by two metres wide and surrounded by garages.

One day, I joined a colleague for a grant-funded greening project that I refer to as "The Triangle." We packed up our snacks, tent, tools, and plants in the car and drove to a SkyTrain station. Confused, I asked my colleague what we were doing there. She said, "This is the site." Looking around, all I could see was the station and platform, the tracks, and a cement walkway over the tracks. I followed her to a triangular spot that was probably only ten metres long and five metres deep at its peak, and was surrounded by a cement wall. "This is it?" I said to my colleague. She nodded. No volunteers showed up, so we removed the invasive plants, planted the native plants, and ate the snacks ourselves.

The whole car ride back I couldn't help thinking how what we'd just done made zero ecological sense. There was no watering system set up, and with the aspect and the cement, it was going to get hot. Those plants were goners. I was afraid to say anything because I was new and young, but it bothered me so much I finally expressed my concerns to my colleague. She said, "Yeah, it will all probably die, and the invasive plants will come back. That's just what we do. We just hope for the best."

In our pursuit of capital *T* ecological Truth, there can only be one path, a singular solution. Eden ecology had us doing restoration in cookie-cutter fashion. Largely the same approach at every site. Now, there are those who will argue with me that their work has been much more sophisticated, but if you really bring projects back to their basic elements, the structure is the same. The singular solution is to get rid of that which we have determined does not belong and plant the things we have determined do belong. All with the purpose of returning to a representation of some arbitrary point in time. Perhaps the time we have determined to be the best version of the forest? I've never been sure. I can't help but think that these colonial notions of the ecosystem are not unlike colonial notions of who Indigenous people are. Notions locked in the past with a hint of mysticism.

It seemed that in our pursuit of the perfect Eden, we didn't recognize that this modern ecology has no choice but to leave humans outside of it. Remember, everything was fine before we showed up. It took me nearly twenty years of my career to finally articulate that. Twenty years of not being able to quite put my finger on why the work we were doing to restore important habitat just didn't seem right. We were leaving human relationship out of it.

The gate was unlocked and opened. As we walked past the "Keep Out, Conservation Area" sign, I looked up the hill at the wondrous sight before me. Towering Garry oaks rose above the sea of flowering camas and chocolate lilies rolling down the hill that was alive with pollinators. I was so moved I simply lay down in the plants. I needed to be with them. To experience what it was like to be them. Then instinctively I dug into the ground to see what the camas bulbs were like. They didn't look healthy. What should have been plump and round were shrivelled and misshapen. Weird, I thought. Then I looked back down toward the gate and thought, Who gets to come and experience this place? Is anyone harvesting these important foods and medicines? No, I was told. It is a conservation area.

There are many excellent reasons to keep the too often irresponsible nature of humans out of important areas. But an Eden ecology of putting things back to "perfection" and leaving out human relationship is harmful to both plants and people. While ecological restoration is important, our work to remedy our eco-logical wrongs has been ineffective over the long term because of the power of the story at its foundation. We have been creating environmental facades eventually doomed to fail without us.

Ecological restoration has become a science where fascinating and exciting work helps species at risk, mitigates invasive species, and illuminates ecological function within plant communities. Despite scientific progress continually informing and improving my years of work in this field, it was becoming clear why we never quite measured up to the daunting task we faced. It was no wonder that I often found myself singing parts of Coldplay's "The Scientist" when I worked, a slightly depressing soundtrack as we found ourselves "running in circles, chasing our tails . . ."[1] Just as my work was wearing on my own heart, the singer laments that science doesn't speak as loud as the heart.

The song is about someone reflecting on a relationship they had and how they might do it differently if they went back, but this poetry can speak to any relationship we care deeply about. Taking the time to reflect on how we might do it differently if we could go back is an important exercise, an investment in trying to do better. Only then can we find the lessons and learn from them to chart a new course. Examining one's own limited perspective is essential for growth, but it's not easy, as I have learned.

What if going back to the start was placing ecology back upon the original, relational foundation of Indigenous Peoples? Perhaps the ecological Truth may be in a relational understanding of multiple truths, releasing us from a singular tether point. Instead, a relational worldview reveals multiple tether points that provide a foundation for weaving together a multidimensional web of greater ecological understanding. We do not discard the wealth of knowledge that has been generated over the history of Eden ecology—it is important to the integrity of the web. As are the stories central to the ecological understanding of Indigenous Peoples. With the freedom of a relational worldview, we have a greater chance of seeing anew how what we know weaves together; we are open to other knowledges and forms of knowledge acquisition. All of which illuminates new paths of inquiry and alternate understanding.

An Indigenous worldview embraces the Great Mystery, allowing us all to exist in a world of small *t* truths. We don't have to have the answers as we are free of absolutes. Our stories are meant to evolve to fit our current reality. They are not one-size-fits-all; their dynamic nature makes them very much alive. There is no need to double down on an old story to assert its relevancy; it is just time for altered or new stories as we learn more. I used to describe my family as dysfunctional for all its complicated dynamics and illnesses of addiction—but that was the influence of the foundational family story. Released of that influence and placed upon a relational foundation of our true identity as Indigenous Peoples, I could see our story was so much more than one of suffering. There were many truths that, when told, revealed new insights and an understanding and compassion I had never had before. The wisdom available from the stories of the past informed us as we created new stories for our family moving forward. The parallel nature of my personal and ecological journeys around the medicine wheel made clear that there is no separation between ourselves and the land when it comes to healing. It's time to write ourselves into the story.

2.

The Missing Puzzle Piece:
The Indigenous Worldview

YOU TAKE your work too personally. I have heard that a lot over
the course of my entire career. So many times, in fact, that it has
become part of my sense of self. I've tried to wrap my head
around this "problem" for years, and worried there was something wrong with me. I've read countless books about work-life
balance and tried in earnest to dissociate from "my work." I have
marvelled at the skill of others to simply hang their hat at the end
of the day. I can't. No matter how hard I have tried, even when
I have clearly told myself, "I am on vacation. I am not working." I
dream about my work. I think about it while I fish or hike or
watch the eagles. I just can never quite escape "ecologist me."
What I have come to realize now is that there is no "ecologist
me." Just me. Indigenous me. That this attempt to separate myself
from my work was just yielding to colonizers, a new form of
dispossession from our lands and from an ecology lived.

In the context of my work, I have cried countless times. Cried when plants I helped to plant died. Cried when invasive plants just won't seem to die after multiple attempts to eradicate them. Cried when I have witnessed environmental destruction resulting from development and poor forestry practices in once-pristine areas where I previously worked. While some of those experiences were utterly gutting, the worst have been the largely unrecognized, less obvious defeats for those of us working in ecological restoration. The worst tears have come in the bathrooms of government office buildings or meeting locations, or after hanging up from a frustrating conference call. The situations where desk-bound policy-makers create regulations that make zero ecological sense. The situations where I would try to talk about important field observations that were worth further research or warranted a change in approach, only to be ignored. Or worse, told there was no way that what I was seeing was happening. The kind of thing that, over time, acted like a vise slowly crushing my spirit.

Tears turned to anger at times, and I lashed out in pure frustration. There was a time when I reported that I was seeing a couple of species along our coastal waters that were only supposed to be able to grow in the dry Interior of British Columbia. Without a doubt, stunted versions of plants I knew well from my summers with cousins in the Interior: spotted knapweed and baby's breath. I was told that I must be misidentifying the plants as there was "no way they would be growing at the coast." I wrote this off as being dismissed because I was young and apparently overly enthusiastic. My inclination to speak up when I thought my knowledge would be helpful, or when I knew an approach was incorrect, or when I felt an issue wasn't being taken seriously enough, earned me a reputation as a "troublemaker."

Around five years into my career, I was working extensively with knotweed species, which are the most invasive plants in the world. They are capable of extensive damage, not just to the environment, such as altering the hydrology of precious fish spawning habitat, but also to infrastructure. This is the plant famous for causing houses to be condemned as it heaved and grew through the cracks in their foundations in the United Kingdom, and for wreaking havoc and causing cost overruns during the construction of the 2012 London Olympics venue, the Velodrome. The species was a game-changer in the invasive plant world. While it is easy enough for governments to ignore environmental impacts of plants, it is much more difficult to ignore those that threaten infrastructure like highways and bridges. I spent a lot of time with these plants in the very early days of their management in BC, helping to try to figure out how best they could be controlled.

In those days, I was told we were dealing with Japanese knotweed and that there was a hybrid out there, Bohemian knotweed, but that there wasn't much of it. The more time I spent with what I was told was Japanese knotweed, the more I realized it wasn't. These plants were the hybrids. They looked different, and more importantly, they behaved entirely differently from the original species. Infestations going for kilometres along the sides of roads seemingly appeared in the blink of an eye. Meanwhile, I would talk with residents about the small patch of Japanese knotweed they'd had on their property since the 1970s. You see, Japanese knotweed spreads only by plant fragments, when living outside its native range. Every infestation is a clone of the original escapees, and the only way it can spread is if the plant is disturbed in such a way that fragments of its stems or roots spread to another area. A disturbance such as mowing is one such example that can chop up one plant and fling it into surrounding territory. Without disturbance, it just slowly expands its circumference over time as the roots work their way outwards from what are very often circle-shaped infestations.

What I was seeing were entirely new shapes of infestations. The appearance of the leaves was highly variable, even within the same infestation. And the way it was spreading, and the aggression with which it was spreading, defied our understanding of Japanese knotweed at the time. When I shared these observations, I was met mostly with shrugs, and told to just keep approaching the management of these plants the same way. Meanwhile, we were getting further and further from achieving meaningful management. These plants were leaving us in the dust. I was left to watch them sweep the banks of streams and rivers that our struggling salmon relied upon. It was like an emergency that almost no one felt the way I felt it.

My own deep sense that something unusual was happening with knotweed came to a head one day when I was sitting under the immense canopy of one of the largest infestations I had ever seen, looking up at the long canes with their distinct bamboo-like nodes, each cane leaning over from the weight of all the foliage at the end. It was as though I found myself in a secret forest in the middle of the city. One so dense that the July sunshine only illuminated the bright-green roof above me, occasionally managing to sneak through tiny gaps made by the shifting wind. As an admirer of plants, I couldn't help but allow myself a moment to marvel at this one. A plant that in its home range is among the first vegetation to grow out of the hardened magma after a volcanic eruption, and here it was, or rather some sort of cousin of that original plant, having morphed to be able to take the Pacific Northwest by storm. I sighed and looked up and down the canes for evidence of anything that might be eating the plants, hopeful that perhaps some insect would be lured by this new, unlimited salad bar and provide us a "natural" solution to tame its onward march. No such luck. My eyes swept along the base of the plants where their canes erupted from the soil, in circular groupings spaced like trees in the forest.

It felt lonely sitting on the ground beneath the cover of the knotweed forest as no one else was with me. I don't mean human relations, but the other plant relations you would ordinarily see. It was kind of a desert beneath the lime green. Or was it? Something caught my eye. Tiny plants growing as though scattered on the edges of the boundary. I got up from where I was sitting and walked over to the edge of the green dome and knelt. There, illuminated by the sun . . . what appeared to be hundreds of knotweed seedlings. You must understand that what I was seeing was supposed to be impossible, akin to saying the sky is silver. These plants are only supposed to reproduce from plant parts; they were not supposed to produce viable seed. But here they were, like children gathered at their mother's feet. Suddenly, the mystifying behaviour of the infestations I had been seeing elsewhere made complete sense. These were different plants that could spread more quickly and farther afield with the help of running water, birds, and animals. The different shapes of the leaves and differences in the plants could perhaps be attributed to this new opportunity for genetic variability that the original clones didn't have. I plucked a few seedlings out to take with me and took endless pictures because I was certain that no one would believe me.

I was right.

I spent a few years trying to convince people running the government's invasive plant control programs of what I observed at the original site and then at many more I found thereafter. Site after site, places where we had been working for years to eradicate what we thought were Japanese knotweed plants, had carpets of knotweed seedlings around the edges of them. I wondered how long I had been completely overlooking and even stepping on them as I worked.

This knotweed experience was one of my first realizations of the power of altering worldview. We only see what it is that we are looking for, or from the lens we are trained and influenced to look from. I wasn't looking for knotweed seedlings because they weren't supposed to exist here. It made me wonder, What else weren't we seeing when we worked in the field? Once we put on this "knotweed-seedling-children lens" they were *everywhere*.

I took a chance and presented my findings at a research conference. After my presentation, I was told by a mentor, "You don't have enough letters after your name." I'm not clear what exactly he was implying—either that I wouldn't be taken seriously without those credentials, or perhaps it was a compliment to the work I was doing. Whatever it was, I resigned myself to the unfortunate fact that he was right, and that I better go and get those letters because my current path of being disregarded and subsequently sent to do uninformed fieldwork wasn't working for me anymore, to say the least.

Eventually, I found that my findings and preliminary work as a field practitioner were taken by academic researchers—they ran with the project, leaving me in the dust. They had the right letters after their names. Why are those letters so important? Why are they a free pass to being believed? I know that I wasn't alone in what I experienced. I watched time and time again as fellow practitioners—those working on the ground in the forest, managing plants—had their deep knowledges and insights denigrated and were themselves personally dismissed over and over and over.

During a speech titled "A Lament for Confederation" at Canada's centennial celebration in 1967, Chief Dan George said: "Oh God! Like the Thunderbird of old I shall rise again out of the sea; I shall grab the instruments of the white man's success— his education, his skills, and with these new tools I shall build my race into the proudest segment of your society."[2]

Done.

THE THREE *RS* OF INDIGENOUS RESEARCH METHODOLOGY
It is difficult not to marvel at how the ancestors have shaped my life's journey. I had no idea how necessary those trials as a practitioner "taking her work too personally" would be to what would come next. I would not be where I am now without that journey. My colonized existence would not have allowed me to feel to my core what it is to have one's land-based knowledge denigrated, dismissed, and attacked. I would never have known that knowledge could be vulnerable to thievery by the very same people who dismissed it. It was a gift of preparatory wisdom. A wisdom in waiting that would give me the strength and determination to stand in front of the colonial forces coming for our Indigenous knowledges now.

Western science has been the cornerstone of my own work; it has served all of us well, and will continue to do so. What I have come to realize is that it is not providing us with the whole picture. Or rather, it may not be providing us with what we need for "big picture" problem solving. Ecology is an incredibly complicated field of study that, like many areas of science, has a myriad of focuses, all locked in dogmatic, encamped positions. The stakes are too high for us to continue placing our eggs all in one basket. The presence of Indigenous Peoples on Turtle Island (North America) for thousands of years, surviving through changes in climate and speciation, and through the attempted termination of our Peoples by colonial governments, is a testament to our qualifications to lead this important work. Adaptation is who we are as a people. We *are* the adaptation experts. So why not turn to us at this time of ecological crisis?

Many are starting to.

Those who previously dismissed Indigenous knowledges are now actively seeking them. Many settler scientists and policy-makers are staring at the puzzle of planetary health and realizing that their lack of progress could be attributed to missing pieces vital to understanding the whole picture. I wish I could find myself freely and fully embracing these new-found relationships. At first, I did. This is what I had been longing for—scientists valuing the knowledges of the Peoples of the land. What I didn't anticipate, perhaps foolishly so, was that just as I experienced with my own land-based knowledges as a practitioner, settler researchers only want to take what we have to offer without understanding exactly what it is they are taking and who they may be leaving behind. Our Indigenous knowledges are being sought with the detachment of a consumer coveting the latest fad. Our Indigenous knowledges are not fads. And there is absolutely nothing detached about them as they are inherently a part of us. We are our knowledges. We are the land.

It is our worldview that makes us different, and this truth often goes unacknowledged. Or perhaps the problem is a complete lack of recognition that we see the world differently at all. This awareness goes far deeper than simply learning some Indigenous knowledge. The trend to incorporate our traditional knowledges into ecology often limits our contributions by treating us as historians and colonizes our knowledges through power imbalances and/or attempts to simply add them on to colonial ways of knowing. It is not okay and, it's plain to see, it is not effective. Traditional ecological knowledge is knowledge shared by Indigenous knowledge keepers. It is sacred. Information acquired from our deep relationship with the places we are from. Intergenerational awareness, passed through lineages about plants, animals, places, and how we care for them. Knowledges acquired in ways beyond that of the physical. Knowledges continuing to be practised and gained, building upon our ancestral understanding. Knowledges generated and their use guided by community values and needs.

There is great benefit to learning and applying our traditional ecological knowledge in a settler's world. However, the full benefit will not be realized without a broader understanding of our relational worldview. To use only fragmented pieces of our knowledge is to admire a tree without admiring its roots. My love of the standing people (trees) is not only in my admiration of their immense beauty, which I can see, but in their foundation, which I cannot. Their beginning as a seed, their extensive roots, the community they are part of beneath the soil that nurtures and stewards them so that they can then make their majestic appearance on the land-scape, their deep connection with Mother Earth, their continued connection and contributions to their communities as they grow. Understanding and acknowledging this is to know the power of the standing people.

Chief Dan George offered his wisdom when he spoke about the integration of Indigenous children into the public school system. I think it speaks to the integration of Indigenous knowl-edge into any colonial structure: "Can we talk of integration until there is integration of hearts and minds? Unless you have this, you have only a physical presence, and the walls between us are as high as the mountain range."[3]

To know our worldview is to know our hearts and minds. To know only our traditional ecological knowledge is to have only a superficial relationship, leaving our knowledges vulnerable to misuse and misunderstanding. You must know and appreciate our roots to understand our real power, our worldview. The head-waters from which our knowledge flows. Only then can you see the world as we do. And by doing this, as Jane Goodall said in her book *Reason for Hope: A Spiritual Journey*, you will be able to "make the old new again."[4]

Is there any better remedy for an old problem than seeing it from a fresh perspective? This is the puzzle piece missing to heal our planet. While the world begins to turn to Indigenous Peoples for solutions to a colonial-caused climate crisis, fragmented bits of our knowledges are being used to fill in perceived gaps of a pre-existing puzzle picture. This "inclusion" is wrong. There is nothing about the overall picture that is just about right when the image itself is fundamentally incompatible with our knowl-edges. The missing puzzle piece is, in fact, the missing lens of a relational, Indigenous worldview. A lens that we need to transform how we see our Earth Mother and all relations and relationships upon it. A lens that stops the chasing of tails and illuminates our collective path forward. A lens that catalyzes new paths of inquiry and alternate understandings.

Imagine yourself putting on glasses. Your first look through the lenses shows you the world as a web of connections that span both space and time. You no longer see things or people or animals as individuals. Instead, it's palpably evident how each of these things and beings is connected to all the others and the environment. You look down at yourself and see your own connections. Your feet to the Earth. Your breath to the trees. Your heart to your grandparents and great-grandparents. You become overwhelmed by the intricacy and abundance of these connections. You are surprised by the relationships you have that you never knew you did. What else do you see? Perhaps you can see for the first time that *you are not outside the natural environment but very much a part of it*. You are in relation with the beings upon our Earth Mother. This is the relational, Indigenous worldview.

Understanding my own feelings of discontent in how I did work in ecological restoration didn't magically disentangle years of learning to ignore my inner voice and be a "good" field researcher. It took years to hone my skills at mind contortion. In many ways, I would punish myself for having these relational inklings, believing my self-worth was determined by the quality of the science that I did. Or perhaps it was the constant reminders that I was a lowly field practitioner that drove me to establish a Western scientific identity in earnest.

My struggle to break free of conventional science made me come face to face with the depths of my own colonization. It turned out it was not something I could simply turn off. It was not so much that it had a hold on me as that I found myself clinging to it. I was already weary, and afraid. I was afraid of continuing to face a career of having my knowledges, and the knowledges of people I cared a great deal about, denigrated. I didn't know what it meant to do ecological research and land healing from an Indigenous worldview, but I knew I wanted to. I had to. It was this poem sent to me by Dr. Peter Cole at the University of British Columbia that gave me the permission to do what I needed to do and provided me a first taste of what Indigenous research methodology is all about:

> write in your own way   think in your own way   research in your
> own way   don't think you have to ask permission   how long
> does that have to go on for   quote your elders   and your
> children   and the wind   the waves   the clouds   they are
> always telling you stories   listening to your stories[5]

Though an Indigenous research paradigm has existed for millennia, it is only in the past few years that it has begun to be accepted in mainstream academia.[6] Our ways of knowing have often been characterized as anti-intellectual. Sean Wilson, a primary voice on this subject, writes:

> The notion that empirical evidence is sounder than cultural knowledge permeates Western thought but alienates many Indigenous scholars. Rather than their cultural knowledge being seen as extra intellectual, it is denigrated. It is the notion of the superiority of empirical knowledge that leads to the idea that written text supersedes oral tradition. For Indigenous

scholars, empirical knowledge is still crucial, yet it is not their only way of knowing the world around them.[7]

From the smouldering ember of having my own land-based knowledges dismissed and disparaged, it was the desire to show the power of Indigenous worldview within ecological research that sparked a new fire within me. My journey was not simply about healing our planet in a better way, it was to unapologetically apply an Indigenous worldview to my fields of study. To show what this offered us all by allowing us to see what we could not otherwise see. To show how to do this in a way that protects our knowledges from assimilation via inclusion. To show "science" that it's okay to acknowledge that we don't need to separate ourselves from our values, spirituality, relationships, and responsibility to community to do good work. That "to do work in a good way" was not just to acknowledge those things, but to centre them. To never lose sight of what we are doing and why. To fight for work to bring healing to our lands to always be personal.

If you find all this strange in the context of science, you should. It is this that sets Indigenous research methodology apart from the Western scientific method—fundamentally, the researcher must be "in" the research. It is the only way that we can then be guided by the three principles of Indigenous research methodology, as identified by Wilson:

Respect   Relationality   Reciprocity

When I see these principles through the lens of a relational worldview, I cannot help but see them in the form of Borromean rings. A Borromean ring is a figure composed of three circles that interlock, forming what is referred to as a Brunnian link. Brunnian links are a set of loops linked together such that "each sublink is trivial, so that the removal of any component leaves a set of trivial unlinked knots."[8] This means that if any one ring is cut, all three rings fall apart.[9]

1) RECIPROCITY   2) RELATIONALITY

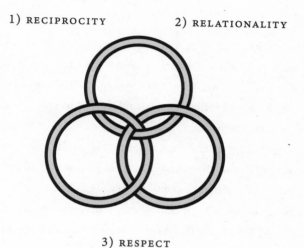

3) RESPECT

The Three *Rs* of Indigenous research methodology as Borromean rings.

Historically, Borromean rings are a symbol of strength in unity. They have also been representative of the interconnectedness of life. All three principles—respect, relationality, and reciprocity—must be part of any research applying an Indigenous worldview. Removing any one principle results in the loss of the entire structure. No two of the three rings are linked only with each other, but all three are linked.

Without ensuring that all three principles remain connected in this way throughout a research process, we lose the ability to claim to have conducted research from our Indigenous worldview. I carry this symbol with me always. It is a check to ensure that I am working in a good way.

What do these words mean in the context of applying an Indigenous worldview to ecological research? How do they help us to ensure that we are doing work in a good way?

RESPECT

Research rooted in respect means that our work must be *good*. Our work must do something positive for the community. This respect places the community in the role of "co-researcher" helping to develop and refine the research question and to determine the objectives, methodology, and outcomes.[10] The researcher must demonstrate respect by being accountable to the relations within the research. Research rooted in respect means that all knowledge is valued *equally* whether it be a story, a vision, oral history, the archaeological record, or soil tests. This concept of respect in research will be among the most difficult to accept by those more familiar with Western scientific methods.

RELATIONALITY

Relationality, the foundation of our worldview, was described above. Our relational connection with our work means that for us, *research is ceremony*.[11] You can consider data collection a series of ceremonies. When working relationally to address research objectives, ceremonies of all types take place. The final ceremony, what Western science calls data analysis, is working relationally with our co-researchers to find the connections between the ceremonies.

RECIPROCITY

Reciprocity is defined in the *Oxford English Dictionary* as "the practice of exchanging things with others for mutual benefit, especially privileges granted by one country or organization to another."[12] This is an important part of Indigenous research methodology as it ensures that our work has a greater purpose than ourselves and that we will always remember why we are doing this work. This is what we, as Indigenous researchers, give back to the community in return for its contributions in this relational effort. Our research must contribute to the community's well-being; it cannot be born without there being a desired community benefit. It is this that makes the work *good*.

These principles are not difficult, and they certainly do not indicate that we are throwing Western science out the window or undermining its integrity. The Indigenous principles of respect, relationality, and reciprocity offer science an integrity found in the relational worldview that is actually freeing.

While the knowledges of Indigenous Peoples may well offer important information within their contexts, our knowledges cannot and should not be taken from us. Healing our planet, our way, isn't about taking fragmented pieces of our knowledges and applying them out of context; it's about the freedom of simply sitting with plants, introducing yourself, and getting to know them in a new way. It is about an unwavering commitment to never forgetting the why of serving community. It is about having humility and openness about where our lessons come from. It is about gaining wisdom to know when to apply which lens and how to bring differing worldviews together. It is about the bravery of making your work personal.

I sat with my teenaged daughter on the porch of our cabin that overlooks the Salish Sea. We had been waiting for nightfall after a long summer day as star gazing is one of our favourite things. We recently found out that she needed glasses for seeing far distances, her prescription nearly matching my own. We hadn't yet gotten her glasses, and as we looked upward in search of constellations and meteors, she was now aware that there was a whole world up there she didn't even know was possible to see before her eye test. She asked if she could put my glasses on. I removed them and handed them to her and watched her intently as she placed the lenses over her own eyes, anticipating what was to come. I was moved by her immediate expression of marvel and joy at a sky she had never seen before. She hadn't known that what she could see with those lenses was even possible until someone offered her a glimpse into that world. She didn't want to take them off. I couldn't stop watching her face, her exclamations both music to my ears and a pang in my heart. I felt guilty that I hadn't known what she couldn't see.

I then looked up at the sky without the lenses I had grown used to seeing through. It was fuzzy and there were far fewer stars. I found even that short time gazing up without my glasses frustrating because I knew what I was missing without them. Then my daughter excitedly pointed at the sky, identifying a constellation she had never seen herself before. I turned my gaze from upward back to her joyous face, illuminated by the moon, beside me. I would never have received this beautiful gift, an important lesson and reminder of what is truly important, if I hadn't handed those lenses over.

Listening to the Relations of the Land

We did not think of the great open plains, the beautiful rolling hills, and the winding streams with tangled growth, as "wild." Only to the white man was nature a "wilderness" and only to him was the land "infested" with "wild" animals and "savage" people. To us it was tame. Earth was bountiful and we were surrounded with blessings of the Great Mystery.
Luther Standing Bear, Oglala Lakota (1868–1939)

We don't save the environment like it is some mission or hobby.
We are the environment.
It is time for Ecology to come home as the salmon do.
To rest upon ways of seeing.
Ways of understanding.
To rest in relation upon our wise Earth Mother.

THE CONTROVERSIAL nature of invasive species and their management cannot be overstated. How we decide which species to manage and how we manage those species can be highly contentious. So contentious that I have found myself being libelled in local newspapers, had people throw rocks at me, been yelled at by strangers, and had the air let out of the tires of my work truck, and a couple of years ago I required police escort to safely get back to our work truck after being stuck on a beach surrounded by a pop-up protest of concerned citizens. People are passionate about plant and animal species, and even more passionate about methods to control them. Especially when such control work is happening in their neighbourhood. I get it. These are tough choices that are often a complicated balancing act of interests. Usually, my work crews and I are the ones on the ground having to do things that are the "least bad" choice.

Invasive species are often defined as plant, animal, or insect species that are not native to an area that are causing harm to the economy, the environment, or human health, or to any combination of these. They are frequently cited as a significant cause of loss of biodiversity. Many of them cause quantifiable harms and must be managed. Giant hogweed, *Heracleum mategazzianum*, a plant from Asia that has invaded coastal BC, is one such species. This species can cause recurring third-degree burns for up to ten years as the skin loses its ability to handle UVB light when exposed to the plant's sap. I have such a burn on the back of my neck from standing in front of the plants during a news interview with the CBC on a windy day. The sap can also cause blindness if it gets in your eyes.

For other species categorized as invasive, their impacts are not so clear, or their impact differs from one context to another, even within the same area. Himalayan blackberry, considered invasive in coastal BC, grows in highly disturbed areas. It provides a free source of food for people, animals, and birds, and grows places most other plants cannot. It can displace native species within what we call "intact ecosystems"—often more remote areas that contain the expected native plant species—but within urban areas, why manage it if it has a food value and isn't bringing other harms?

Eden ecology operates by what I refer to as "dichotomously led" ecological restoration, one that asserts a static view of ecosystems: native species good, invasive species bad. It has left no room for nuance, or for circumstances where invasive plant species may offer some benefits to other native species. For example, the flowers of the invasive spotted knapweed, *Centaurea stoebe*, running along the decommissioned railway behind my own farm are often covered by many species of pollinators, including honeybees, many of which are struggling where we live. This plant can indeed be problematic on ranch lands and in meadow habitat, displacing other species, but in this location, I struggle to see the importance of managing it. We are far from such places, and this old, decommissioned railway is full of invasive plant species because of its history of being highly disturbed. It's surrounded on each side by dense forest, habitat that these invasive plants cannot live within.

One summer, the railway-adjacent plants were such a spectacle of pollinators the sound of them was like a motor running on a truck. I went out to record this and my daughter asked me, Why would anyone spray these weeds here if they aren't causing any harm and the bees like them? This may seem a simplistic perspective coming from a child, but it is a worthy question to ask. It is the exact kind of question I would never dare ask in the company of my peers. I work in a field of study that is unforgiving of the wrong opinion. The stakes are high, whether you are a practitioner or a researcher, for even opening up a conversation about justifying why we may be managing a specific species deemed "invasive." Any such conversation is perceived as an undermining of our unspoken mission to maintain the perceived purity of ecological systems.

The bottom line is that the "native species good, invasive species bad" system of categorization isn't perfect. It allows for no consideration of changes in climate or climate adaptation. When trying to heal lands, actions are often not context specific. Our ecological restoration plans are often predetermined before we even set foot on the site. A cookie-cutter approach: kill what does not belong (invasive species) and replace it with something that has been given the status of "belonging" (native species).

I believe that the widely held position of my professional community—that invasive species must not be tolerated, full stop—may well be reactionary to the position of "live and let live" for all species, held by equally passionate naturalists. It seems there are two, and only two, widely polarized and divisive answers to the question, What species belong?

That is, unless you ask an Indigenous knowledge keeper.

LUSCHIIM:

What is a knowledge keeper? Well, for me, some say I'm a knowledge keeper. But I say I know very little compared to the old people. But I remember. Children were shooed away when people were gathered together. Children were told, "Go outside and play." I'd go to the door, and I'd sit down, and I'd slowly come back. Slowly come back. I'd crawl under the table. I'd be listening to the words that were coming out so . . . Many times I'd just go up to an Elder and sit with them. I'd see an old man sitting there. Especially [name omitted for confidentiality], I'd go and join him. I didn't really know him.

I knew him but not . . . Of course, after several times, he started to talk and he started to share stories with me. So it became quite broad what he shared with me. So I learned from just sitting with him. Not asking for it. Just being there. I find myself the same way if somebody comes in, joined me several times, I will share things with them. Maybe it's come from their own great-grandmother. So that's how you become knowledgeable. Just by listening.

That's a real important bit. Learn to listen. When I was talking about me crawling off the table, under the table, that's what I was doing, I was listening.

So, I listened. I sat with Elders and other knowledge keepers in offices, in oceanside camps far in the bush, in nature preserves, in sacred places, and in Tim Hortons. And I listened. Listening can be difficult when we feel as though we have an agenda, like a research question to answer. The stories and knowledges shared with me, the conversations I had with my new friends, felt all over the map at first. In the beginning, I felt frustrated that we never seemed to be talking about my desired topic. It is difficult for me to admit this now; in fact, it makes me feel ashamed. I try to forgive myself for those early days of being wired by the colonial world to be quick and efficient and laser focused. I didn't understand yet that what was being given to me through this sharing and conversation was far richer than a simple answer to a one-dimensional research question formulated by a Western scientific worldview.

Had it not been for my own journey of cultural reclamation happening at the same time as my graduate work, I think I would have remained stuck in these mind-prisons of single-tracked thinking, valuing efficiency over everything. I realized that the vast knowledges I was being given were like pieces of a grand puzzle—each piece necessary, each to be collected in its own time. I relaxed, cleared my schedule, and embraced the many times when one coffee turned into three, or when I didn't make it home for supper.

It didn't matter that we weren't always talking about invasive species or ecological restoration—sometimes we talked about how we teach children, how we care for our Elders, or archaeology, or a hockey game. It was about building relationships and talking about anything from an Indigenous worldview. A worldview that is relational. I was learning how to embrace the relational thinking that had always been within me, and how to practise it. It became clear to me that whatever topic of conversation I got to be part of, ultimately, we were talking about direct and indirect relationships with land and each other. It started to seem silly to me that ecology could be considered a singular topic or silo of scientific study. Its definition—the branch of biology dealing with the relationships of organisms to one another and to their physical surroundings—made sense, but in practice within ecological restoration, this was not what I experienced. The entities involved in these relationships weren't given the kind of consideration they should be when we are trying to help bring ecosystems back to a healthy state. I don't really recall as a field practitioner ever having specific discussions about relationships between things like the soil and plants, or spending time in quiet observation just seeking out important relationships that could inform our actions. It seemed mostly like superficial acknowledgement of certain relationships and blindness to or wilful ignorance of others.

I was starting to understand that to connect head and heart, my task was to collect and put these puzzle pieces together, guided by each of the teachings of the medicine wheel, my own experiences, and the knowledges (Indigenous and Western science) I carried. All to create something that would help us to bring healing to our land, our way. It was a puzzle without the picture on the box to guide me, but it was becoming clear that the puzzle would reveal what it was that we needed to know, what an Indigenous ecology looked like.

My original, and somewhat embarrassing, initial research question acted as the catalyst for what would eventually emerge:

What are our Indigenous perspectives on invasive species and their impacts?

It would be much easier, neater, and tidier to say that I could provide a definitive answer to this question. Spoiler: there isn't one. What I've encountered on this journey is a series of answers found at various places along the middle of the "philosophy of invasive species" spectrum. The answers were not static. Like the nature of our Indigenous stories, they could adapt and change depending on the context. There was a beautiful and reflective fluidity to it all. A vast departure from absolutes and dichotomies. This fluidity created an openness and respect for all knowledge sources that I had not come across before.

LUSCHIIM:

I observed when I was two years old. I was living it already. Wasn't that much, but it was a beginning. Three, four, growing, growing. Names of things, names of places. And then I can see obviously more detail later on. My great-grandpa died just before I was six. So in that, three years old to just under six, I learned a whole bunch off him, lived a whole bunch. And that just kept growing from there. How do I know [a plant is] useful? We were shown different plants. One day somebody might come and want some.

How would we know what would be useful to us? I think I explained that at the beginning. I live it. So. How do I know? I don't know how to answer. It's 'cause I live it.

Growing up away from my own traditional territory, I was never exposed to place-based knowledge in an everyday, tangible sort of way. There were places that I had worked for many years that I knew very well, but I know now that it is not at all the same. I think back to time spent on Tsleil-Waututh lands with my Tsleil-Waututh friends. I always had deep admiration for how they knew every piece of their land so well. When they showed me things, it was like being let in on precious secrets. Something I still hold close to my heart.

Indigenous knowledge is so tied to place. Those ties are not just about familiarity, but relationality. When you care for land that takes care of your family, that is a relationship. Something I have always longed for as an Indigenous woman displaced by the colonial history of my family. I am fortunate enough to work with Indigenous communities close to where I live now as well as those farther afield, and am grateful to be a witness to their relationships with their lands. I am grateful to have permission to have relationships with those lands and the Peoples of them. But I am still a guest and behave as such.

In our modern, global world, fewer and fewer non-Indigenous people live in the place that their ancestors did, while so many Indigenous People still do. Land inseparable from identity. Knowledges that span thousands of years, passing along through our ancestral lines. Knowledges older than those acquired through the Western scientific method. Knowledges that often informed and continue to inform scientific inquiry. Elders have described to me many times how their own Elders would show them plants growing near where they lived so they could identify them, and then describe to them where certain plants could be found growing farther away where it was appropriate to harvest. They would then be sent out onto the land from the time they were young and, using those descriptions and familiar landmarks, they would find and then harvest the plants and bring them home.

For me, respect of knowledge shared by Elders and community knowledge holders is easy. I have been taught this since I can remember. What I have been most afraid of is how to fulfill my own responsibility as a knowledge holder and eventually an Elder. While I can listen and hold as much knowledge as I can gather, I have often wondered, How do we continue to acquire important knowledge? How do we know things and how do we determine what is important to pass along to the next generation? At some point, someone had to figure out this knowledge that we have continued to pass along.

As we continue to adapt to our changing environment, it seems so important to not just carry the knowledges passed down to us, but to know *how* we continue to acquire important knowledge. As a plant knowledge keeper myself, I am particularly concerned about this. Have we lost valuable abilities to assess plant use? Have I walked so long in the colonized world that I do not have this ability? Or if I do, am I brave enough to have faith in it? I asked Luschiim about this.

JENNIFER:

What if, in this scenario, you came across a plant that you'd never seen before that nobody knew? What would you do to decide whether it was something that was useful or something that, really, you wouldn't want to have around? How would you determine that?

LUSCHIIM:

Couple of things there. I didn't like school. I had no use for it. How could I use this knowledge and learning at school? That's what I thought at that time. Why do I need to learn social studies? I don't need to learn about Germany or Australia or anywhere. Japan. So we used to play hooky when come time to sit in subjects. One was social studies. Other one was English. Other one was spelling. I didn't need that. So we'd jump out the two-storey window from the school. Go up the mountain. I see plants. I didn't know I was studying plants, but I'd see plants I didn't know. I'd describe them to Grandpa or Granny or my mom or dad. And they'd kinda guess what it is. Eventually we'd find one and I'd say yeah, that's what I saw up there. Then little did I know I was learning where they were. And when somebody needed it, I knew where they were.

School-age me would have high-fived Luschiim and taken the lesson as saying I didn't need to go to school. I know Luschiim well enough to say he certainly is not devaluing the importance of an education—*but*, what he is saying is that there are different kinds of education, and they are not equally valued in Western society. How are we to research and describe relationships if we do not know them personally? Experiential, land-based learning, time with knowledge keepers, access to knowledge keepers, are all important pieces of education. Academic institutions need to respect the important contributions of knowledge keepers and provide space to them within these institutions so that students, Indigenous or not, have access to them. We must respect these knowledges by recognizing their existence, valuing them equally to other forms of knowledge, understanding them in relation to the Indigenous worldview, and stressing their importance as the foundation of any study of ecology at any level. Science education delivered in this manner not only provides a richer and more complete picture of ecosystems, but it can act as the catalyst and nurturer of lifelong relationships between people and the lands where they live.

Our knowledge holders are not limited only to our human relations. There is much to learn from our animal relations, and an Indigenous ecology embraces lessons from such teachers. To learn these lessons, we must be open to them. We must spend the time with these relations to get to know them well enough so that we can see what they are trying to show us. We have to respect them as teachers, not simply research subjects. Animals hold valuable knowledge that can be shared with us if we listen. Many knowledge keepers have told me to watch the animals, they help us to find the medicines.

LUSCHIIM:

So here's one other story. This guy is walking on a trail. Way up the mountain there. There's a good trail. I mean a larger trail. Animals, people always used it. Elk. Someone or something stepped on this snake and it was injured. Just laying there injured. This guy picked up that snake, put it on the other side to get it out of the way, out of the way of the trail. Some time later he was coming back and he's like, "Ahhh, I'll go look." He's looking at that poor snake.

Some chewed-up leaves on the grass where it was. Looking ooohhh, I don't know how much later, it was the next day or what, he's coming by to look and it [the chewed leaves] was there. The snake was gone. He looked a' it several times. Then he got right down to look at it to see which kind of leaves they were. So that is one of our good medicines. She was showing what to use. So I learned that story early in my life.

———————

Our knowledges are rooted in our deep connection with our land, now referred to as our traditional territories, and the relations that inhabit them alongside us. The boundaries delineating these territories were drawn after colonization; they outline where our communities largely resided and the land that sustained us. The very existence of these maps implies that we largely stayed within these boundaries, but that is not the case. Indigenous People travelled, often to trade goods and resources, sometimes for great distances. It is critical to acknowledge this as part of our history as it is foundational to an Indigenous ecology.

One noticeable light bulb moment for my non-Indigenous friends who have taken a keen interest in my research journey is this new understanding that Indigenous people travelled extensively hundreds and thousands of years ago. They realized that they had this notion that we didn't go very far, and they didn't know why. This led to further discussion about versions of history that they had been taught in school, which were more about fur trading and the Hudson's Bay Company than about the lives and history of Indigenous Peoples before colonization. Seeing my friends—Indigenous allies—have these revelations and reckon with their own colonial misperceptions has been a genuine privilege.

These false perceptions and their origins are important to acknowledge as they continue to contribute to the legacy of colonialism. Many are not even aware of their own colonial interpretations, past and present. For my friends, it has taken discussion with me, an Indigenous woman, to recognize it. It isn't really their fault. The dominant society educated them this way and continues to reinforce these false ideas about Indigenous identity and Eden ecology. What they do with this realization is up to them, as it is now up to you. You can see how these perceptions, no matter how small or insignificant they may seem, inadvertently permeate and influence the structures we participate in throughout our lives, whether they be in government, in our jobs, what we study, how we study. This is how colonization has had, and continues to have, an influence on our understanding and application of ecology. We need to make a purposeful choice to stop it.

LUSCHIIM:

All I can say is we travelled. What I was told, we travelled to what is now called Kamloops, what is now called Chase, for trading missions. California. Off to the other side of the big river down that way which means the Columbia River. Sometimes we went way further.
Sometimes it took two years to make a trip. So how far did we go? You know, Mexico has stories of people arriving. I have a Mexican son-in-law. His family has got some stories. How far do you travel? Depends on how strong you were . . . We travelled a long ways.

I got asked, Did you guys travel to Alberni? Well, we know of the trail that went from Kwalikum, which is Qualicum today, over the hill and to Port Alberni. But also from Cowichan Lake, into Cowichan Lake down a valley into Alberni. And I'm told—I'm told that the

*oak over there, the DNA says it comes from Cowichan. I don't have
backup to that, but that's what I was told. Mm hmm.*

The travellers carried fish eggs, shellfish, plants, and seeds with
them. Just like modern travellers, we also brought pieces of home
along with us, brought gifts for our hosts, and participated in the
exchange of goods through commerce. While it is true that
the invention of more efficient modes of transportation since
that time created a truly "global" existence, Indigenous Peoples
had an "international" existence long before colonization.

The global nature of our modern-day existence is often cited
as a major factor in the spread of invasive and non-native species
into new ecosystems. While modern transportation has certainly
hastened and extended the reach of plant life, it does not negate
the often ecologically forgotten fact that species were moved
around long before colonization. Species have been moved for
thousands of years by Indigenous Peoples. This calls into question
our foundational notions of concepts such as *nativeness*, the very
dichotomy guiding restoration ecology. We must respect the true
history of the land as an Indigenous ecology requires it. An
Indigenous ecology acknowledges the changes on the landscape
as a result of our travels far from our own territories hundreds
and thousands of years ago.

The history of the Garry oak ecosystems in coastal BC is a
testament to the influence of such journeys. Typically located
on Vancouver Island, they are the ecosystems where the Coast
Salish grew bulbs like camas, the primary source of starch, for
food. A friend doing Garry oak preservation was telling me
about a small outlier population of the deciduous trees on the
mainland of BC, east of Vancouver, on the Fraser River. He

shared that there had been debate about the origin of those Garry oak trees: Why were they at this critical and prominent place along the river? The answer seemed obvious to me. They were given to the tribe there by a visiting Nation, or the tribe there visited the island and brought them home. Perhaps for as simple a reason as because they liked them. Perhaps they symbolized a relationship between Indigenous Nations. Both a discussion with Luschiim about trading between Cowichan Tribes with my own Nation from the Lytton area, and a study of the genetics of this population, supports this.

LUSCHIIM:

So Yale, Hope and Yale. Yale is the beginning of the canyon; of the narrow part of the canyon. So I went to Yale one time to do an interview. I was working for a research outfit, and they were hired to go do interviews over there. So we're doing our work, [interviewing the] oldest people up there over that time. We had a big meal. So during the meal, we're finished our work, I asked the oldest man up there, I said to him: "You know, I'm told we used to go to Kamloops and Chase." And he took us down to the river to talk about the river in that place. And I was looking at the river, how swift it is, and I'm wondering how we made it up. So he just chuckles, "Oh, we knew when you guys were coming. We built walkways. Had them up the cliffs. When you guys arrived, you guys rested for a few days, and we would pull you guys up. You switched places. And everybody done it, all the way up." So that's what he told me.

And then when he finished that part I said, "I understand that we got mountain goat wool." And he chuckled again, "Yeah, that's right. Your guys went up. Your young men went up and got 'em. We just sent our young guys to show you where the goats were.

*And that was that." Then he finished off by saying, "We looked
forward to those times. You guys also fished and put away a lot of
fish, pink salmon, sockeye. But here's what we liked about those
times: When you guys went home, you left us big canoes.*

Indigenous Peoples' economy and protocols have always had an
impact on the land, a fact that upends the construct of the
"natural" environment. The concept of *natural*, as in "natural
area" and relatedly "natural environment," is a colonial social
construct when we consider it within the context of Turtle
Island. These concepts are rooted in the perceived "wildness"
of the "New World" "discovered" by settlers; a perceived wildness that did not recognize the work that went into what were
highly productive and managed landscapes.

These often romantic notions of "nature" represent another
piece of the foundation of modern ecology that has no place in
an Indigenous ecology. An Indigenous ecology respects the true
history of our land by acknowledging our relations that shaped it.
Settler perceptions of the apparent "naturalness" of our forests in
coastal BC are so deeply embedded in modern culture that our
province's tag line is "Supernatural British Columbia." I know
that I am not the only Indigenous person who finds this somewhat amusing. While our province is certainly beautiful in a way
that feels mystical at times, I have grown up knowing that our
ancestors shaped this landscape to meet the needs of our people
in many of the very places that people admire as "natural." This
perception of a natural state is fundamentally important as it is
this notion that drives our modern-day Eden ecology.

While it is understandable that settlers more familiar with
agrarian landscapes would see our forested lands as unproductive,

nothing could be further from the truth. Indigenous communities worked to ensure that our land and waters were productive enough to support us all year long. We lived this way for thousands of years. What we see on the land and water today—the various tree species, berries, rock formations in the intertidal zone—are in many cases the remaining legacies of that hard work on the landscape; legacies often unacknowledged and taken for granted. In most cases, this is attributable to simple ignorance of the nature of our relationship with the land and the impact of our ingenuity upon it. I don't blame settlers for not knowing this. Even as an Indigenous woman I didn't know about some of our land practices. Almost every day I walk past a clam garden (midden) and a fish trap, and I didn't even know it until my friend Tom showed me. Now that I know, they are blatantly obvious to me on my coastal travels.

There is so much we don't know because we haven't wondered why things are the way they are, instead working off the colonial assumption of this inherently "natural" landscape. In fact, care for our relations is essential to an Indigenous ecology. Our bringing balance to the ecosystem includes practices of preventive care for all relations (humans included). Often it involved managing the genetic diversity of all our relations. A practice so common and important that there is a word for it in the Hul'q'umi'num' language, *Hwteyqnuts-t*, which describes the intentional movement of living things such as plants, trees, and clams for this very purpose. Hwteyqnuts-t was an essential traditional stewardship practice to ensure the health of the relations relied upon; one that has been described to me in every Indigenous territory I have worked on. One that is being revealed through historical ecological methods and modern genetic analysis of our plant foods such as hazelnuts.[13,14]

Elder Peter Williams, of Cowichan Tribes, shared with me:

Well, at the weir site, they dug holes in the riverbed. From each species, the spring salmon eggs would go in one hole. Then the coho eggs would go in another hole in the riverbed. And then the kw'a'luhw, which is the chum salmon. And then the steelhead. S-xuw'q'um'. They would put the milk from the male from each species where it belonged for each species. And my dad used to be up there.

From plants to fertilized fish eggs, desirable species for food, medicine, and ceremonial purposes were moved between communities. Bentwood boxes of fertilized fish eggs were moved from one stream to another both to enhance fish stocks and, as Elder Peter Williams put it, "to set the table." Plant communities were influenced by the manipulation of species composition, density, and production timing. All acts of reciprocity, so that all relations may thrive.

LUSCHIIM:
Say we went down the river and scooped out the eggs, into a container. "To take it," punum; "to go plant them somewhere else," punum; "to plant or sow," punum. So there were two words: punum and hwteyqnuts-t. So we go punum eggs. That's the word that we used for moving the eggs is punum.

And the old stories. This old lady told a lot of it. She was born in 1873 and she died in 1974 according to her headstone. She said, Sometimes your daughter or son ended up in a place where there was no or hardly any salmon. And we punum. Take some from home, home stream somewhere.

Our relational worldview places us within the ecosystem, and our importance within it is demonstrated by these preventive land-care practices, meaningful acts of reciprocity. As we have lost our direct connections with the land, as our food systems have moved us away from the land and into grocery stores, what becomes of our relations such as the salmonberry or the thimbleberry? Our modern Eden ecology may take for granted the presence of these "native" species on the landscape, but without a human relationship, what becomes of them? As many of these species disappear from the land, it becomes clear that these plants need us if they are to continue. Thinking relationally, we must take this even further—what becomes of the birds and the bears that rely upon these food sources?

Knowledge keepers have described to me stewardship techniques to allow for continuous harvesting, such as cutting back berry plants in the spring so they would produce later in the season to ensure a continuous fresh supply of fruit. Others described watching the plants to see when the soils needed amending. Evidence of when the land would get sour, such as when berries would start to get small and other plants that liked acidic growing conditions, like rushes, would appear. In Hul'q'umi'num' the word for land needing to be burned is *sa'yumthut*.

The landscape that we see today was purposefully shaped by our ancestors, not just for food and medicines, but for technology. We have found opportunity in species that arrived after contact, and we utilize them as both food and medicine just as we did with climate-driven changes in speciation over the thousands of years of our existence along the Salish Sea. Western red cedar, which arrived approximately five thousand years ago to coastal BC and which could have been considered an invasive species by modern evaluation, is now foundational to our coastal Nations' identities. Adaptation defines who we are as a people.

A story that Elder Luschiim told me about Scotch broom— a species long known to be a pervasive invasive species on Vancouver Island, and one I have spent many hours managing over the years—demonstrates the fluid nature of our Indigenous worldview on belonging.

LUSCHIIM:

You know, how did we acquire the knowledge about Scotch broom? That's a very good medicine. It's beat medicines that the doctors gave. Some of the things that were bad that it was used for . . . a fertilizer or what they put on strawberry plants. A lot of our people ended up—their skin just kind of melted away and weeping. And that it would spread. Just started weeping. My aunt, she's still here. She was picking berries when she was young. That's probably in the thirties. Twenties or thirties. And it [her skin] got really bad. It was weeping and she couldn't pick anymore. We used to go to the States, Washington, to pick berries. Strawberries or raspberries. So she got sent home 'cause she was just costing money when they're just feeding her. Money was really scarce. Everybody had to earn their keep. She wasn't earning her keep so they sent her home. So the grandpa, one of the grandpas, heard about it, his granddaughter been sent home. He come to see her. He looked at her. Went and got that Scotch broom. Kept boiling water and cut that Scotch broom put it there. Pour it. [motions with hands] Washed her up. Within a few days she, she started to heal. From that Scotch broom.

How did we find out? I don't know. I couldn't answer that. But there are many medicines like that. That came by, by sight, or a vision of some kind. A dream. How do you say that to somebody,

*like in a government? You know. Would they believe it? The things
that some people can see. There is no explanation.*

It is not to say that we do not acknowledge the negative
impacts that these species can have. This perspective is not one of
"live and let live." Luschiim shared with me some of the negative
impacts of Scotch broom and Daphne laurel causing medicines
to disappear in specific areas.

LUSCHIIM:

*It's wiped out a lot of our natural vegetation such as a flower, some
of the flowers that we use either as food or medicine. Um hmmm.
Like up on Mount Tzouhalem. Where the onions and where the
chocolate lily is. You know, there's no more there. And some of the
places where balsam root used to grow, it's all just Scotch broom.
So yes, it does cause a lot of problem.*

This point of view demonstrates the departure from a strict
belongingness dichotomy of Eden ecology. Indigenous ecology
has a more specific type of belonging, one where we have the
freedom to decide whether a species belongs in a given place based
on the relationships of that species in that place. This is an extension of our worldview, where we see ourselves within the system,
and where it is okay to influence the system to meet the needs of
all our relations in it. Our own needs included.

The invasive blackberry species on coastal BC emphasizes this
point. I was once managing this plant around the swiya (lands) of
the Shishalh Nation, the Indigenous Nation in the area known
as the Sunshine Coast of BC, and a couple of Elders came out to
speak with me. They knew that the plant was invasive, but that

they managed it near their homes so they could pick it as it was a source of food they enjoyed. They asked if I could please leave it. Which I did. Many people, Indigenous and not, in coastal areas enjoy this free source of delicious berries. Making it one I am never keen to control unless absolutely necessary. Elder Mena Williams once told me that many invasives are used for foods and medicines as well. I have been asked to collect species such as St. John's wort, comfrey, and burdock many times by Elders.

An Indigenous ecology, resting upon a foundation of relationality, means that acts of reciprocity are inherent within it. Our ecology is not separate from acts of stewardship but is, in fact, lived stewardship. Respect for the land and acts of reciprocity are not for the greater good, but a fulfillment of one's responsibilities within our role as the balancers of our Earth Mother. Our stewardship is an act of love between relations for all relations, and it is not bound to definitive concepts of belongingness of species, nor to aesthetic concepts of nature. It is practical and it is respectful. Its legacy has shaped what we see today, and our departure from it shows a legacy being lost in real time.

These acts of reciprocity, respect for our relations, were not simple transactional acts. They were much more than "this for that." The depth of our understanding of the fish, animal, and plant relations we relied upon made reciprocity our way of being, part of everyday life. Acts such as moving plant, shellfish, and fish species from one place to another, sometimes great distances, are important examples. We may be inclined to point out how interesting it is that there was a recognition that genetic diversity was important. Many I have shared this with have done so. But to express that is to depart from the humility required to embrace our Indigenous ecology. We were not primitive people. Our terminology was and is different. Our methods of knowledge acquisition were and are different. Science may help us to understand the nuances of these acts we were once freer to do upon our lands, but scientific discovery is not synonymous with knowledge ownership. Our living stewardship was and is purposeful.

As our time in the northern direction of the medicine wheel comes to a close, we leave behind the colonized ways of trying to help our planet and carry with us the teachings and wisdom of our Elders, knowledge keepers, animal and plant relations, and the land. We take their teachings with us as a spark to see how an Indigenous ecology, resting upon a foundation of relationality, provides us the freedom required for solving the ecological crises we face around the world. Within it we are free to embrace epistemic openness, work without absolutes, welcome all knowledges, and value the truth of the land.

I carried with me the teachings of the Elders I spent time with and of the land and felt as though an Indigenous ecology had been fully revealed to me. I believed that I had connected my head and my heart. The spark of the North had ignited a fire beneath me, and I walked this journey more confidently, sure that we were on the right path. If that were the case, the book would end here. It's funny how the ancestors seem to have tricks up their sleeves. Colonial chains are hard to break, and I didn't realize that I remained tethered to them. Perhaps it was the mercy of the ancestors that such a fire be lit beneath me before the most difficult work began. The spiritual work in the East awaited me. As it does you.

Part Two

Spiritual Journey to the East

IT IS time to move to the eastern direction of the medicine wheel. A place where new journeys begin with the spiritual work to connect us to the land so that we may release ourselves from our current ways of knowing and doing. Changing worldviews is more than simply flipping a switch.

4.

The Unravelling of Protectionism

Change is hard.
Even when you want to.
Even when you know it's the right thing to do.
Sometimes the beginning of a journey is an unravelling.

I pick my way along. Making my own path around the rocks and roots and ferns and shrubs and trees, on the hunt for the plant invaders. The target set. Fixated on the glowing red dot on my iPad map. I have done this long enough that little attention need be paid to my surroundings. I brought my best friend along to assist. Her first time out on such a quest. As I moved swiftly, homing in on the bad plants whose demise was imminent, she kept asking me, "What is this?" pointing at the surrounding flora. Ordinarily such inefficiency would make me annoyed, but for some reason, her curiosity intrigued me. With my recent pondering on worldviews, I realized that her curiosity provided me a rare opportunity. Often, I am working with folks who, like me, have spent most of their lives crawling through the dense brush. It isn't so much that you take it for granted as that you just don't take it in anymore in its entirety. So I tried to patiently answer her questions. And then I realized, I didn't know the answer to a lot of her questions.

I looked around through her eyes and finally saw all the plants, the shrubs, the trees, the mosses, the insects, the fungi. I felt like I needed to introduce myself to them. How was this possible? How did I not know many of them? The ones I did recognize felt mostly like acquaintances I'd met in another context but couldn't remember where. Later, I realized that we met when I placed checkmarks next to their names on lists from native plant nurseries. I had some old friends I could introduce her to, though. The berries I ate with my dad when we fished the rivers and creeks, for example—but those were awkward introductions as I couldn't remember their names. They were mostly typecast as edible or not.

I quickly became overwhelmed by this surprising sense of unfamiliarity. I felt as though my feet left the Earth. Disoriented. Quickened breath. I glanced down at my iPad and realized that the glowing red dot was within my crosshairs. I looked up. There they were, right where the sun broke through the canopy. The invasive knotweed plants. I breathed a sigh of relief, feeling grounded again. There you are. My enemies. Thank goodness.

In this moment, I realized that my way of seeing the world had become so reflexive that it could have been part of my autonomic nervous system. Years of conditioning by my education, experiences, and profession had moved me far past simple indoctrination. I was hard-wired to see that which *did not* belong.

This realization occurred just as I had embarked upon my journey to see my work in ecology from my heart—my

Indigenous worldview—rather than my head, all before figuring out how to bring the two together. I was shaken as it revealed just how single-minded I'd become—not just in how I saw the land and the plants, but how "Team Western Science" I was. In my immediate self-reflection, I was shot back into my memory of a PhD committee meeting where it was suggested that I transfer from Plant Science to Interdisciplinary Studies. It felt as though my work was being downgraded from "real" science to, well, something else less good. Western science was my identity, one I carried and had never confronted before. An identity that, at the time, I was unaware was already unravelling as I stepped into my Indigeneity. This wasn't just about my work. This was about me too.

Freeing myself from my head was not going to be as simple as flipping a switch. I was going to have to do some preparatory work first. I had to retrain myself away from this reflexive way of seeing, but this is easier said than done. We are built by what we know. The values we are brought up with, the stories we are told, the education we receive, and a lifetime of experiences all shape who we are. Who we are creates the frame from which we see. As we progress in our careers, whether they be in academia or not, we develop confidence in this frame and our ability to use it analytically.

It is at this point of relative life experience where we transition into what is referred to in my culture as young Eldership. We carry valuable experience and knowledge and it is our time to share what we know with others in our community. This life stage is both an honour and a privilege, but it's not without its own challenges. We have learned and seen so much that it becomes difficult to approach problems from a new vantage point, even when our knowledge may fail. This is the folly of the modern-day "expert." Let me be clear: This is not a devaluation of expertise, but an important observation deserving of dedicated awareness. As I found in my own experience, the wealth of knowledge born of my education and experience in invasion biology and ecology made it difficult to see things from an alternative world-view. A worldview that lay within my DNA that I had intense personal desire to "see" from.

While I have certainly received a quality scientific education, the culture surrounding it set the stage for me to simply turn off the Indigenous part of myself in the name of conducting sound science. Working in ecological advocacy and education, I became rooted in the dogma of our field of study by the strength of the hyperbole I used as an effective tool for communicating the invasive species cause. Any possible glimpse from my Indigenous worldview was fleeting at best.

As I worked to plan a large invasive species conference, I was hoping to bring in Dr. Ken Thompson, the author of the book Where Do Camels Belong?, *as a guest speaker. In the book, Thompson considers examples of the contradictions of "native" and "invasive" species and the crucial questions about why only certain introduced species are successful.[15] He is openly critical of how our fears could be getting in the way of conserving biodiversity and responding to climate change. I was encouraged to read the book by my colleagues in Alberta during a work trip and, after doing so, felt personally challenged by how it mirrored my own professional self-doubt. Every invasive species conference I have been to has had speakers from "our camp," so to speak, so the opportunity to bring in a new perspective that would stimulate debate over the course of the conference seemed exciting. Sadly, as I eagerly presented the idea to others involved in the conference planning, I was not met with shared enthusiasm. The criticism? "He's too controversial." "His views are too oppositional to our own."*

In retrospect, my suggestion of this speaker should have tipped me off that I didn't quite belong. That said, I aligned myself within the prevailing culture of invasion biology that is oppositional to alternative perspectives. I rolled my eyes along with keynote speakers who flippantly cited the work of the common detractors in a theatrical manner. It seems that the biologist Mark Davis has also experienced this as he said, "There are times when invasion biology has not been as welcoming as it might have been of diverse perspectives."[16]

The very nature of science is that it is a constantly changing, self-correcting process, which evolves along with advancement of knowledge. This suggests that alternative perspectives which challenge current theories should be welcomed. While there can be resistance to paradigm shifts within any field of study, the strong aversion to alternative ideas within the field of invasion biology seems especially pronounced. In his acclaimed book *The Wisdom of Crowds*, James Surowiecki wrote that "the mean of a group of independent estimates is generally much more accurate than any single estimate. However, if the group acts as a committee, it usually yields a much less accurate estimate than the mean value based on independent estimates of each individual of the group."[17] He explained that the poorer performance by the group when operating as a committee is because the small-group dynamics reduce the impact of independent thinking in the group.[18] It seems evident that the invasive species community is largely operating by committee-level thinking. This is concerning because, as Davis said, "Like all sciences, if invasion biology

is to maximize its progress, it needs to encourage diverse perspectives, to be open to criticism, both from inside and outside
the discipline, and to effectively network thousands of indepen-
dently minded researchers and managers."[19]

The commitment to prevailing theories, even when empirical
data have contradicted them,[20] is not likely unique to invasion
biology. These examples within my own fields of study show that
we must acknowledge the reality that it may not be the science
itself that is holding us back from being open to the application of
alternative perspectives; it may well be the cultures surrounding
the fields of scientific study themselves that are holding us back.
So often these cultures have arisen in defence of the integrity
of the fields themselves. A noble and important cause. However,
if the defences are stopping alternate forms of understanding or
even new preliminary paths of inquiry, I can't help but be worried
about what we are missing out on. Especially at a time of ecological crisis when we need untethered human ingenuity and
innovation. These cultures can be so aggressive that they disincen-
tivize "outside-the-box" thinking. Professional risk becomes too
great to venture down unexpected paths and thus, those paths are
left unexplored. I allowed myself to be conditioned by that culture, perhaps even doubling down on my subscription to it to
compensate for what tugged at my heart. I feel badly about that.

In an age where inclusion of diverse voices is increasingly a
priority for research institutions, the preparatory work for providing healthy space for underrepresented voices in STEM is
not being done. Scientific fields of study must be open to the
new ways of seeing and understanding that diverse folx bring to
them. Being unsettled should be expected and prepared for.
This is what is required for meaningful confrontation of factors

influencing the accepted Truths in their field of study. Inclusion on its own is not enough; along with inclusion can come harm to those voices as their approaches are met with skepticism, dismissal, and worse from those perceiving their work as a threat to scientific integrity. I have avoided joining conventional Western scientific societies related to my fields of study for this very reason. My heart can't take it. It isn't because I cannot defend my work, it is because too often I am unable to fully communicate the work without defensively being cut off. Too often the criticism becomes personal, especially since separating my identity from my work is not a privilege I have as an Indigenous scientist. The preparatory work that needs to be done is the unravelling before the building of something better. The unravelling that will give scientific fields of study the freedom to not put someone like me in the numerous unfortunate positions I have been put in.

I think we have all found ourselves frozen by fear of expression of original thought. It is a fear rooted in the potential of facing ridicule for questioning the prevailing consensus and a fear of being ignored. Within the academic setting where I now find myself, I cannot help but wonder, Does this fear provide the context for us as researchers to freely push the bounds of our knowledge and understanding? Academic institutions operating within the dominant paradigm have become a "safe space" for understanding and discovery. Safe so long as one yields and subscribes entirely to it. The result is a risk-averse culture where we do not make the waves the world needs for fear of drowning.

It may seem like it, but I am not beating up on Western science itself. It has provided us with a way to formulate important research questions, find reliable answers, and build upon the work done by others. It serves an important function. It has a role to play in the acquisition of knowledge and progress of society. My criticism is that this paradigm has a culture that has morphed it into an ideology of academia. The *only* acceptable ideology of academia.

Discussions with non-Indigenous academic friends have revealed similar feelings and frustrations. It is ironic that they have shared that I am in a better position to push back against it. I suppose upon reflection it makes sense because as an Indigenous researcher I am more directly affected by its limitations. I have no choice. My way of knowing simply cannot be made to fit within the dominant paradigm.

The purpose of the application of the Indigenous worldview to research is not to generate alternative perspectives on current scientific understanding. Nor is its application a simple exercise of integration of traditional knowledge into Western scientific methodologies. *The application of an Indigenous worldview pushes us into an entirely different world of research.* Using Indigenous research methodology, we depart from research confined by the guise of objectivity. There is freedom without risk of persecution to explore new ideas, other methods of acquisition of knowledge, and how we arrive at our conclusions. We can create work that is the realization of the potential that comes from the unchaining of researchers otherwise bound by the rules and culture of the dominant, Western scientific worldview.

The protectionist culture of any field of scientific study and the defence of their cornerstone, the dominant paradigm, are to be expected. The question is whether this self-protecting culture of dogmatism is best serving the interests of the academy and society.

5.

It's Time for the Time of the Eagle

I married a non-Indigenous man who came from a small German/
Mennonite family. A family whose culture and size greatly contrasted
with my own. His culture is best described as one of formalized structure,
understood and unspoken rules (which are always followed), and quiet
peacefulness. I think it was quite a transition for him to be shot into my
extremely large and even louder family. Kids running around playing,
squealing, and generally having the run of the place. Adults telling each
other like it is. We might as well have been from different planets.

When he observed parenting in my family and community, he saw
chaos. When I observed parenting in his family and community, I saw
stifling childhoods.

We carried these biases with us into parenting our own children. It
took a few years of disagreements to realize that what we were
experiencing was a culture clash in our own home.

He feels strongly that children need structure and rules. I observed in
his family an imposing of familial social expectations from a young age
and the consequences of departing from what was expected.

I explained to my husband that in my culture, we recognize that children are in the time of the eagle. A precious stage of life when you are the closest to the Creator. Parenting is a ceremony where we guide our children toward the fulfillment of their life's purpose. As guides, it is so important to let them be free during this time of the eagle. A time for self-exploration. A time of building foundational relationships. To allow them to find and embrace what it is that makes them uniquely themselves and to discover their gifts. It is by no means a free-range scenario, but one that is filled with aunties and uncles and cousins keeping an eye on their physical and spiritual safety without unnecessary constraints.

Honestly, the debate between our cultural parenting styles has still not been resolved, and given that our children are 15, 15, and 13, it probably never will be.

When I think about the colonial world today, one that often rejects, marginalizes, and romanticizes (sometimes all at once) Indigenous worldviews and knowledges, I think about this parenting debate. It may provide the best analogy for what we are currently experiencing under the dominant paradigm. *We are living a stifling childhood mired in constraints.* We need to embrace and experience *the time of the eagle.*

While we may have been brought up with different cultural parenting approaches, I am happy to report that my husband and I both turned out okay. We are both smart and productive members of society. If we are evaluating the results of our own cultural upbringings based on the above-mentioned attributes, can we say that one type of childhood was better than the other? On the surface, the answer must be no.

But:

Perhaps it is our obsession with this very question that is the problem. We must move away from the question of which is better and instead ask, What is the result of a childhood where two different cultural parenting approaches are utilized? While this experiment is far from over, preliminary results do seem worth noting. Our children are a tangible demonstration of what happens when two differing worldviews are given an equal platform. They are heading out into the world with much more open, accepting, and fluid world*views*. Plural. They can see the world in two ways and aren't afraid to express this apparent superhero capability. They are fearlessly creative and naturally push back against the ordinary and conformity. They think critically. They know how to change how they see the world when problem solving and see the benefit of being able to do that. My children are already fulfilling an important role as intercultural knowledge bridgers.[21]

Our inadvertent cultural-clash-parenting experiment shows us that the real work is in providing space for both worldviews. This involves the creation of the context for a shared and equal platform to exist. I find it amusing that such a context may be easier to create within a marriage than in the place I find myself within now as an Indigenous academic. My husband and I came together because of our mutual respect and appreciation for each other (including our differences). Something that, at least through the lens of social media, we seem to be losing as a society in general. I experience the proclaimed intentions of folx every day to embrace "otherness." Sadly, more often than not, such intentions are not manifested if "other" does not play by the rules most of society are comfortable with.

To create room for multiple worldviews, the dominant worldview has to yield to provide space. As an Indigenous academic,

I can tell you that in my experience the burden of space creation has solely been mine to bear. I will also tell you that once you work your way onto the platform (often elbows up), it doesn't mean people want you on there. I have personally experienced this lack of mutual respect and appreciation. I once had a mentor try to talk me out of my current research project because "that Indigenous stuff would undermine [my] credibility as a scientist."

Let that resonate.

This upward battle to establish credibility is difficult and can seem threatening. Sometimes it feels as though it would be easier to just give up. This is where it is going to take a commitment to understanding, mutual respect, and a heap of humility for mainstream thinkers in order to help us find an easier way up and to provide the support we need to remain there.

We proudly share our parenting platform. It may appear equal, but my husband has a distinct advantage. He practises the parenting approach most others are used to. If he is out in the world with our kids on his own and they are running around causing a disturbance, others nearby will give him the benefit of the doubt. Maybe it was time for the children to run off a little steam. If I am out in the world with our kids and they are running around causing a disturbance, others nearby are likely *not* to give me the benefit of the doubt. The kids are running around because I am not parenting the right way.

This is what it is like for Indigenous academics. Even when we find a place on the platform, we must constantly defend ourselves. We do not have the advantage of the benefit of the doubt. We are often not acknowledged at all.

Throughout history, scientists and funding agencies that support their work have dismissed alternative knowledge systems as insignificant when they have contributed to the development of "modern science." As Europe was "discovering" the new world, for example, "ethnobotany and ethnozoology were established to grapple with the sudden influx of biological information from 'foreign parts.' . . . Western science profited from the appropriation of traditional taxonomic and ecological understandings, with little acknowledgement of their intellectual origins."[22]

Indigenous knowledge is a scientific paradigm. *Science* is defined in the *Oxford Learner's Dictionary* as "the intellectual and practical activity encompassing the systematic study of the structure and behaviour of the physical and natural world through observation and experiment."[23] You will see similarities with the definition of Indigenous knowledge. I will use the definition provided by Nakashima et al. in their *UNESCO Sources* article "Tapping into the World's Wisdom": "Indigenous knowledge is the local knowledge that is unique to a culture or society. [It] encompass[es] sophisticated arrays of information, understandings and interpretations that guide human societies around the globe in their innumerable interactions with the natural milieu: in agriculture and animal husbandry; hunting, fishing and gathering; struggles against disease and injury; naming and explanation of natural phenomena; and strategies to cope with fluctuating environments."[24]

In order to have mutual respect and appreciation for our differences and discover our similarities, we must get to know one another better. Here, Indigenous researchers take a turn at having the advantage. We have been living in and learning the dominant paradigm of Western science since grade school. We learned about the scientific method, its history, and how to apply it. We know more about you than you know about us.

Think of when you meet someone for the first time. Your first impressions are not based upon a thorough understanding of the person and their context. They are based upon a snapshot of your experience with them. I have several people in my life who, when we first met, did not make a favourable impression on me at all. My grandmother always said that there was good in everyone, so you must give everyone a chance long enough to find that good. She was right. One of these very people is my best friend in the whole world now. A woman whom I initially mistrusted, but now admire deeply and try to be more like.

We often say we need to build bridges of understanding. Such a statement may be to put the cart before the horse. Who wants to build a bridge to somewhere you don't know much, if anything at all, about? I realize that as much as Western, colonial society needs to make space for me, I have work to do to help those space makers get to know our Indigenous worldview. Lack of understanding is the perfect recipe for misunderstanding. Most of the criticisms I hear and receive about decolonized and Indigenized research practices are quickly resolved when I begin sharing about applying this worldview to ecology. Improving understanding is the first step to reveal the potential of our way of knowing to bring healing to our planet and to compel the spacemaking we need our allies to do.

My daughter Alicia had to give a presentation about Indigenous women in leadership for school. I was honoured that she chose me, even though I had suggested others, but I found myself struggling to then explain to her what I do in a way that would make sense to her and her classmates. Becoming impatient with my hemming and hawing, she said, "Mom, what makes your science different than everyone else's?" I love how kids have a way of cutting to the chase.

That was an easy question. I said, "How we learn the stories of our lands, waters, and relations is different than Western science. Basically, the way I do research breaks a lot of the norms and rules of the science designed by the colonizers." With a clever smile forming on her face, she said, "The wrong way?" Chuckling at this characterization of my life's work, I said, "Yes, Alicia. Proudly, the wrong way." I couldn't help but marvel at her inference at the age of fourteen that wrong meant anything that didn't follow Western scientific methods. Guess her time of the eagle was made shorter by her colonial education.

Objectivity is revered in science. A necessity for research to be considered valid. The thing is, working as though research is actually objective and denying the often personal reasons that drive us to do the work we do is, as Eber Hampton said, "a goddam lie, it does not exist."[25] I have a hard time thinking of a single person I know working in ecological restoration or conservation who isn't motivated to do the difficult and often thankless work they do by their obvious passion to care for our land and waters. Perhaps we would all benefit from being able to be truthful in this regard. I can't help but wonder if scientific research would be more believable and trusted by society at large if we were transparent about our motivations.

I found such relief that subjectivity, the influence of our own personal beliefs or feelings, is *expected* in Indigenous research. In my own experience, when I have looked to Elders to help me with research projects, their first question is usually, Why are you doing this work? What makes it good work?

Who is a researcher? I think when I was a kid I thought researchers were scientists wearing white lab coats looking into microscopes. While when I went to university, I became much more aware of the diversity of research areas—and their associated attire (not white lab coats)—but I still thought that the work required honorifics like PhDs. Even if the researchers were wearing plaid and standing in forests. I had even allowed myself to take the title of "Practitioner" during my years of doing "trials" as we worked on learning more to control invasive plant species. There was no way I allowed myself to think that pre-PhD me was doing research. I was so incredibly wrong. I will first qualify this by saying that it is important to ensure we value and honour the knowledges of experts, something that has perhaps become eroded in today's public discourse. However, experts don't always work in universities; they don't necessarily have university educations. They don't even have to be adults. I have spent enough time on land with Elders, knowledge keepers, and land guardians (who include teenagers) to know that my time with them has resulted in more learning than I received in a classroom. This is *why they are my co-researchers* and part of a cumulative and collaborative analysis of findings.[26] A time of the eagle means that we need room for *all the researchers* to be in our circle.

I have always found it difficult to develop a hypothesis for a research project, even when I was in high school science. A common critique of my research questions, then and now, is that they are too broad, too unfocused, and that I am trying to do too much. I have felt bad about this for a long time. As if it was some sort of personal failure. It wasn't until I started working on ecological restoration alongside Indigenous communities that I realized the problem wasn't me. My relational way of seeing, my

Indigenous worldview, made the connections and relationships—between land and water and plants and the two- and four-legged and the winged—my grand focus. I was drawn to and could not ignore the inherent connectivity of our ecosystems. My relationality wasn't the problem; it was the siloing of science that wasn't working for me or our ecosystems.

With such a relational focus, we need the space to be able to ask these questions that might seem too big. We also need the space to then ask questions that might seem weird to most. Robin Wall Kimmerer in *Braiding Sweetgrass*[27] presents the differences between the questions asked by Western scientists versus Indigenous people. While she was doing her undergraduate degree she found that when encountering a plant they didn't know, "the questions scientists raised were not 'Who are you?' but 'What is it?' No one asked the plants, 'What can you tell us?' The primary question was 'How does it work?' Research subjects are reduced to an object." Recently, while working to control an invasive grass species in an area where Roosevelt elk lived, a few colleagues' eyebrows were raised when I vocalized a question to some of the elk as they passed us by: "How do you know this grass?" In a meeting among Indigenous co-researchers planning a wildfire restoration project, a knowledge keeper asked, "What plant medicines do the animal relations need?" Our focuses are different. Our questions are different. We need the freedom within science to work this way.

Just as the questions we ask may be different, how we answer them and how we determine the validity of those answers is also different. Indigenous knowledge is not gained in a lab or even in books. It is acquired through the passing down of cumulative knowledge over time through stories and experiences. We must understand something with our whole being—mind, body, emotion, and spirit—to truly know it. The emphasis is only on mind and perhaps body when training as a Western scientist.[28] The validity of these knowledges and ways of knowing is a constant target and justification for their dismissal by defenders of Western science. A time of the eagle would give us the space to create bridges of understanding regarding the validity of our knowledges. They need not be justified by the Western scientific method, though so often they are, as an Elder recently reminded me: upon my own lab learning about the germination of a culturally important plant, he laughed, "Yeah, I've been telling you this for years now."

Now, we were not testing this because I questioned what he told me; we were trying to learn more based on what he told me. For me, this is exactly how our differing worldviews can work to support each other to generate better science to inform land healing. I think it's important to understand that we have our own standards of validity of our knowledges. First, given the importance of accountability to our communities, there is great risk in asserting something that isn't true. Second, not unlike standards of colonial education, no one simply self-stamps themselves as a "knowledge keeper" of anything. That is a title earned and recognized by community for the knowledges given to, earned by, and carried by that person who then has the responsibility that comes with such knowledges. To put it bluntly, this is not like your uncle who has googled something and spouts off on a topic and calls himself an expert. Far from it. Specific knowledge keeping often passes down through specific families, each playing their important role in carrying knowledges that contribute to the collective health of the community.

———

We cannot talk about healing our planet without talking about Indigenous languages. It is not just their animacy that changes how we relate to our environment. The more words I learn in different Indigenous languages pertaining to lands, waters, stewardship, and food systems, the clearer it becomes that they are like keys, unlocking important knowledges of the past. The more we reclaim and revitalize our languages, the better able we are to fill gaps caused by colonization, particularly those that go beyond the memories of our surviving Elders. The meaning of words can provide instructions for land stewardship, describe plant care and plant genetics, and tell us of the acts of reciprocity as part of harvesting. Our science requires there be space to include the preservation and revitalization of our languages. Something so often thrust solely into the category of social sciences by the colonial silos of Western academia. I cannot help but grieve for what has been lost—often within one generation—while at the same time feeling heartened by what we still have.

In my own family, I recently learned that my great-grandfather was fluent in Secwepemctsin. My great-uncle heard him speak it, but my great-grandfather *never* spoke it to his own children. While many of us do not speak our languages fluently (I'm trying to learn!), the ways we have been taught to relate to our world by our Elders are so often rooted in our languages. There is power in a science that can stop objectifying the relations we share this planet with, while teaching us how we can effectively balance ecological health with the needs of all relations. We may need to adapt some of the stewardship practices we learn from our languages to fit within the modern context, but it is the deepening of our understanding of our ecological responsibilities that will enable us to act upon them with the tools we have today.

Transitioning to a scientific time of the eagle sets the context for us to build the bridge between the Western scientific paradigm and Indigenous worldviews. Scientists from the dominant paradigm will have to acknowledge and move away from the tendency to defend their ways of thinking and doing simply because that is the way things have been done over the course of Western scientific history.[29] There have been paradigm shifts in Western science before; I'd like to think that a more inclusive version is yet another.

There is great potential for each paradigm to be able to credibly inform the other. As American philosopher Helen E. Longino writes, "There is general agreement that in order to maximize opportunities for progress and breakthroughs in disciplines based on collaboration, it is vital to accommodate diverse perspectives."[30] As she emphasizes in *Science as Social Knowledge: Values and Objectivity in Scientific Inquiry*,[31] a primary benefit of participating in a diverse community is that the community is able to recognize and cancel out the biases an individual brings, either intentionally or unintentionally, to the table. When we are working to heal lands and waters that have belonged to Indigenous Peoples since time immemorial, and colonial history and sciences are relatively short in time scale compared with that, the importance of plurality in ecological thought is clear.[32]

It is important that we ensure that informing each other is done in a respectful fashion. Caution needs to be exercised as too often it seems that Indigenous knowledge integration has merely become a fashionable trend amounting to little more than a box-ticking exercise. In some ways it has become what I describe as the shape-shifting of colonialism and it has led to a new form of extraction by non-Indigenous people. It is critical that a scientific time of the eagle, a time for making the space for our worldviews and knowledges, does not lead to the dispossession of our (Indigenous Peoples') knowledges.

It is my hope that we can build bridges in research that, as Kimmerer suggests, allow differing knowledge systems to work together but remain distinct:

> The Three Sisters offer us a new metaphor for an emerging relationship between indigenous knowledge and Western science, both of which are rooted in the earth. I think of the corn as traditional ecological knowledge, the physical and spiritual framework that can guide the curious bean of science, which twines like a double helix. The squash creates the ethical habitat for coexistence and mutual flourishing. I envision a time when the intellectual monoculture of science will be replaced with a polyculture of complementary knowledges. And so all may be fed.[33]

There are already examples of both paradigms credibly informing the other. An excellent one is the migration of the eastern Chukchi Sea beluga whales. Harvests from this stock form an important part of the diet for the Inupiat village of Point Lay, Alaska.[34] While the Inupiat hunters were able to provide researchers with "extensive traditional knowledge of the ecology of the belugas in the Point Lay area, they offered no information on the subsequent movements of the animals" when they left the coast.[35] The hunters "expressed great interest" in having this information, and worked with scientists using satellite telemetry to track the belugas' migration.[36] This is a great example of how Indigenous knowledge and science can work together to more accurately complete the picture.

My goal is to not only provide another example of how our Indigenous worldview and science can work together successfully, but to share my journey so that others may see themselves in my own struggles. So that they will come along with me, realizing the potential of existing in a scientific time of the eagle that is free to embrace other ways of understanding and knowing. A freedom that can only be possible with humility and bravery from us all. A freedom only possible with open hearts, grace for the many mistakes that will be made, and patience as we all learn to navigate this time of the eagle together for the greater good.

I had a dream one night in the midst of my struggles to figure out how to bring together what often seemed like diametrically opposed knowledge systems.

I was looking for a weed and was being drawn deeper and deeper into the forest. The light became dimmer as I walked and even though I knew that no weed would be living in this darkness, I kept walking deeper and deeper into the thickening bush. I wasn't scared. I was being drawn toward something, but not so much that I couldn't turn around. Suddenly the smell of something burning hit my nostrils. Who would be having a fire around here? I thought. I continued walking, the smell of the fire intensifying with each step. I was stopped in my tracks when I came around a bend and saw a giant boulder across the worn-down path. Now I could hear the crackling of the fire, which must've been just on the other side of it. There did not appear to be any way around this giant boulder. As my eyes adjusted to the increasing dimness of the setting sun beyond the dense cover of the forest, I could see that one side was a steep gully; the other side impassable as the boulder was wedged into the side of a hill covered by what appeared to be a spiky, thorny thicket of bushes I could not recognize. The call of the fire at this point was so intense I could not turn back. I moved closer to this giant obstacle and stood, looking up at its immensity, frustrated that I could not see how to get around it. The light of day rapidly fell away such that I could now see the sparks of the fire swirling upwards on the other side. "Hello?!" I said loudly to whomever I assumed to be tending the fire. My voice echoed back to me off the boulder. The only response was the continued crackle of the flames.

There was no moon and eventually I found myself in complete darkness. I approached the boulder, stepping into the thick, tall grasses that grew out from its base, reaching out until I touched it. It was still warm from the passing day. I ran my hand along it, feeling for what, I'm not sure. Perhaps a new way to orient myself in the darkness. I crouched into the grass as I ran my hand down the surface and then my hand disappeared into grass, seemingly swallowed up by the boulder. I snatched it back. As it seemed to be unscathed, I reached back into the grass, feeling around. There was a small opening at the bottom of the boulder that I hadn't seen before. I got onto my hands and knees, reaching forward in the darkness, pushing grass over to create a path as I crawled. I reached up and felt the boulder above my head. I was in, or rather under, it. This was the first time I felt fear. And then, as I flattened aside more of the lushest, densest grass I had ever encountered, my eye caught the flickering light of the fire between breaks in the grass. The light began illuminating the tunnel I could now see that I was in. I crawled toward the glow and began to feel the warmth of the fire.

Finally, I emerged into what appeared to be a hidden, circular, outdoor space surrounded entirely by boulders. The fire burned in the middle. I stood up and looked for the person tending to it, my eyes scanning the perimeter aglow. No one. I looked at the fire. There was something different about it. I walked up to it, transfixed. The flames were a multitude of colours, intertwining and dancing together but never *seeming to blend. They interacted yet remained distinct. Each colour made me pause and admire its beauty. I did not have a favourite. One colour took the lead and then another and then another. I was filled with a sense of wonder. It was fire, but it wasn't. I didn't want to leave it, though I got the sense it was time to go. I consoled myself with the fact that I could return when I wanted. I now knew where the hidden opening in the boulder was.*

6.

Bringing Ceremony to Science:
Lessons in the Weeds

ENTHUSIASM CAN be a dangerous force. Our Elders teach us that slow, careful, considerate, and purposeful preparation for anything is key. I have learned that this shift in paradigm, one where we learn to use multiple worldviews, should not be as simple as flipping a switch, nor should it be rushed. It should be more akin to a slow wading into unknown waters.

This preparatory work has two important purposes: first, to free ourselves from the confines of colonial perceptions, and second, to prepare our hearts to work within a worldview that must include spirituality. The latter is often thought to be the most difficult for a modern scientist. However, this is not what I have found. As soon as I remind colleagues of the feelings of marvel and awe they may have at their work or even as they take in a breathtaking view, they recognize those feelings and experiences as hints of the spiritual world that we too often cut ourselves off from in the name of rationalism.

It is important to understand that this spirituality is not associated with the dogma of a particular religion, nor is it the mysticism that too often accompanies colonial notions of Indigeneity. It is spirituality grounded in gratitude for all relations and relationships. It is an honouring of those who came before us, are here with us now, and will be in the future. It requires of us the service that comes with practising reciprocity. It is a spirituality that is secure in the not knowing. It is the energy that feeds our whys. It is the summation of all that the dominant worldview demands detachment from in the name of practising good science. A detachment that creates a facade of objectivity. We are all not so different—the difference is simply pretending that working with such detachment is possible. Perhaps this is why it is not so difficult to embrace an Indigenous worldview after all. It is the truth we all long for. It is a relief to work this way. To work in service of our whys.

It would be a lie for me to say that I knew exactly how to give up control to allow myself to see afresh. Feeling inclinations to work from both Indigenous and Western scientific worldviews was a lot different from knowing how. There were no instructions on how to do it. Everything written was theoretical. As I walked one morning with my dogs through the trails amongst the standing people, I went back to the teachings of the eastern direction of the medicine wheel and mulled how they could help me begin to translate theory onto the land. The morning air seemed to transport me back in time to precious memories with my father before he passed.

There were many mornings where I would wake up before the sunrise and sneak out of the cabin with my dad to go fishing and catch the morning bite. As difficult as it was to get up so early, there is something sort of magical about that time before the sun begins to rise. A stillness in the air that holds the last bits of the evening's moisture. A silence of anticipation. I remember bringing towels to the boat to dry off the dewy seats. Only the sound of the gentle bumping of the boat against the dock as we placed our rods and tackle and snacks in it. Then we got in and sat tying our lines, as if to draw out the silence a little longer before we broke it with the hum of the boat motor. It was often a silence-breaking tie between the start of the boat motor and the single call of a loon across the lake.

As we headed out to our fishing spot, the first hints of the sun appeared behind the mountains, and the water began to turn from black to a deep purple. It was still difficult to see much ahead of us in any detail, but there was enough light to spot any hazards in the lake. I dragged my fingers through the passing water as I watched its colour change with every minute through the palette of purples. We arrived at our spot and cut the motor to the increasing songs of birds and the sounds of splashing fish jumping and rolling, the light still too dim to see them. It was like existing in this gently expanding cocoon of seeing that was comforting rather than disorienting. We dropped our lines just as the first pinks of the rising sun revealed the detailed outlines of the trees at the top of the mountains that surrounded us.

The insects began to appear, flying over the surface of the lake, which was now a mirror of the beauty around us. It was difficult to know which way was up, and I made a game of looking back and forth from the reflection to the horizon. As the sun rose, we could feel the warmth of the day ahead. This is when we broke out our snacks from the cooler. Sometimes we had caught a fish by then. The occasional eagle flew over to see if we had an easy breakfast for it to steal on our lines. As the sun climbed higher, the splashing of the fish began to dissipate. We brought our lines in and headed back in a sea of dragonflies as they seemingly patrolled the lake alongside us. We could hear the echoes of voices over the water as the rest of the community began to rise for the day. We tied our boat up to the dock with the smell of bacon and eggs in our noses. Before heading up to the cabin, I always turned to the water and admired the view that was so different from when we had headed out only a couple of hours before.

It's funny that when you are in need of a lesson, a memory comes to you that shows you you've already learned this lesson. It's like being handed an instruction sheet for your current problem. All those years, getting up early, crawling past all the other sleeping kids in the cabin, the lure of the ceremony drawing me outdoors in spite of my sleepiness. That's what those mornings were, a ceremony. It was hard to get up that early, but it gave us an entirely different experience of our surroundings. An experience that altered our perception and sense of time. Time was told by the changing light, the order of emergence of our winged and finned relations, all signals other than our watches.

There was a rhythm to the ceremony. The time with my dad was so special—just me and him. It was the specialness of these mornings that made me take in every one of those details so that they would last a little bit longer, so that I could remember them and return in my mind whenever I liked. The passing years of that ceremony continued to reveal new details, new ways of seeing and experiencing the lands and waters around us. I remember now, actively looking for a new detail each time, seeking something I had not seen before.

We yielded to the lack of light. My dad was adamant that we not use a flashlight when heading to the boat in the early hours. He'd say, "Just give your eyes a minute to adjust. You can see what you need to. Just be patient." Boy, how I wish I could talk to my dad and thank him for this lesson now. At the beginning of this journey, I already had my answer to how I would give up control and see anew. I wasn't going to fight or force what I couldn't see yet. I realized that what I needed to know or learn from this experience of learning to see the land from an Indigenous worldview was not going to be served up to me in one helping on a silver platter. I had to take my time, embrace each detail as it was revealed, and find beauty in the process. In making this a ceremony, I could no longer be controlled by deadlines, or by my colonial sense of productivity. This was about intentionally creating opportunity through ceremony to see things differently.

The first ceremony for me was to speak truth. I had to speak my truth to provide clarity for what I was about to do, and to release myself from the dominant paradigm. I did not want to have to continuously apologize for or explain through my own research journey that I was not working from a Western scientific worldview. If I did that, I would only be perpetuating the notion that Indigenous knowledge acquired through an Indigenous worldview was lesser and needed continuous justification. I was well aware of what I was doing, so I would speak my truths and carry on forward in ceremony. Unapologetically.

The following were my statements of truth as I released myself from the constraints of the dominant paradigm as an Indigenous researcher:

- I give myself permission to stop attempting to create the illusion of objectivity.
- I give myself permission to stop attempting to distance myself from my work.

- I give myself permission to openly express my personal connection to my work.
- I give myself permission to not engage in the game of knowledge ownership.
- I give myself permission to not ask whether how I conduct my research is the correct way.
- I give myself permission to embrace discovery in whichever way seems right.
- I give myself permission to learn lessons however they may arise.
- I give myself permission to learn from all who cross my path.
- I give myself permission to defend my work from colonization.
- I give myself permission to stop engaging in processes that require me to legitimize my work.
- I give myself permission to stop softening my work to make settlers more comfortable.
- *I give myself permission to not be afraid of the repercussions of producing work outside the dominant worldview.*

To these truths I remain committed as they are the foundation I stand upon as an Indigenous researcher. They are here for me as a reminder to stay true to who I am. They are here for you as a reminder that colonization has a continued grip upon the lives of Indigenous people and that we must make daily, purposeful efforts to free ourselves in the many facets of our lives.

The concept of "the beginner's mind" was raised by my PhD supervisor, Dr. Carol McAusland, after I discussed this ceremony with her. Unfamiliar with this concept, I found that it was a subject area worthy of further attention as it provided clarity in explaining the process I was undertaking. Shunryu Suzuki in

Zen Mind, Beginner's Mind says, "In the beginner's mind, there are many possibilities, but in the expert's there are few."[37] The term *shoshin* is a word in Zen Buddhism that means "a beginner's mind" and "refers to having an attitude of openness, eagerness, and lack of preconceptions when studying, even at an advanced level, just as a beginner would."[38] This is a concept that is somewhat at odds with the position of nineteenth-century scientist Louis Pasteur, who said, "In the field of observation, chance favours the prepared mind."[39] A position that best describes the context required for the "aha" moment of a scientist. Only through a "prepared mind," acquired through extensive education and experience, could the conditions required for discovery be met.

Just as I had found in my own process of attempting to leave behind the Western scientific worldview to embrace an Indigenous worldview, Mark and Barbara Stefik observe that "as we work in an area, we gain experience and acquire particular patterns of thinking. A mindset is a pattern and a set of assumptions that guide our thinking. Over time, these patterns of thinking become deeply ingrained. Without noticing it, we become very efficient at thinking 'inside the box.' When we're faced with a novel situation, these built-in assumptions can cause us to overlook inventive possibilities and potential breakthroughs."[40]

I think it may be difficult for some experts to see the value of contributions a "beginner's mind" can make toward our own fields of study. A major hurdle is a culture of defensiveness of our own position within our fields for fear that a beginner may undermine our contributions as experts. I personally experienced the devaluation of the "beginner's mind" early in my career as perhaps many of you have. I recall countless times when, as a newly working invasive species specialist, my comments beginning with "Why don't we just . . . ?" or any other attempt to offer alternative possible solutions were quickly dismissed by more senior government staff. These experiences were quite deflating and incredibly frustrating.

Now that I am more senior myself in my professional community, I understand the tendency for this type of disregard. Beginner-level thinking can lend itself to an inefficiency we don't necessarily have the time for. Very often these suggestions have been tried before without success, or require a budget we just don't have, or are impractical for some other reason. All things a beginner doesn't know yet. Out of the despair I felt in those early days, I attended a seminar on "multigenerations in the workplace" to help me better understand the disregard I was experiencing. While I left with a better understanding of the dynamics, I refused to accept them as a work culture I was willing to tolerate. I vowed that if I became an "expert" at anything, I would be open to the value a beginner might well bring to me.

My own beginner, out-of-the-box thinking gave rise to new strategies for invasive species public awareness and education campaigns that were recognized internationally for their successes. But to gain attention for my ideas, I had to go around the experts rather than finding someone to listen and help me. The effectiveness of what I designed didn't bring praise from those who should have been there to help and mentor me. Instead, it made me their target. Situations that led me to embrace the saying: "The mighty oak was once the lone nut." Perhaps it was this personal experience and the promise I made to myself that made me inclined to revisit the "beginner's mind" once more.

What I have come to realize is that the prepared and beginner's mindsets are relationally connected and play important roles in the progress of any process of knowledge acquisition or discovery. The answer to the question of whether a "beginner's mind" or a "prepared mind" will lead to important breakthroughs or discovery is that both can. Further, both mindsets can reside within an individual. While some have suggested that an expert seeking to take on a "beginner's mind" should "discard your previous experience,"[41] I see it instead as the expert setting said experience aside temporarily. It is about the creation of the mind-space needed for an expert to realize the potential of taking on a "beginner's mind."

Mind-space creation requires a conscious effort to set aside what ordinarily occupies that space. This was the intention of the mental exercises I completed within this research journey that I will share in the pages to come. While I will never be able to be a beginner within my fields of study again, and I may not be as likely as a beginner to come up with a completely out-of-the-box discovery, I can use my knowledge and experience to find and address the weaknesses within my field of study by bringing together both the dominant and alternate worldviews.

The process of breaking out of a prepared mindset can be extremely difficult. For me, it was a matter of being open to experimenting and figuring out strategies that worked. In their article "The Prepared Mind versus the Beginner's Mind," Mark and Barbara Stefik present strategies and exercises to help with this process, including changing activities, trying the opposite, and uncovering assumptions by discussing the subject area with someone unfamiliar with the topic at hand. Retrospectively, I realized that I had used these strategies they described in their work in my own "ceremony in the weeds," which I will describe later in this chapter. I found their analysis to be a reassuring after-the-fact discovery that my own intuition was correct.

The adoption of an Indigenous worldview, to me, was more than a simple adoption of a "fresh perspective." To work from a different worldview is to embrace a new philosophy. Something that affects both perception and the interpretation of those perceptions. In my mind, to fully realize the potential of a new worldview, the deep work of dedicated ceremonies was necessary. This involved a significant investment of time. We do so much work investing in the creation of a "prepared mind" through our years of education and experience, I think it a challenge to experts that time be invested, at the appropriate career stage or when a unique opportunity may arise, in the creation of a "beginner's mind." There is much to be revealed by what we presume to know already if we embrace the "prepared beginner's mind."

Achieving this mindset was a process of release; a reorientation that could only have come through both "unseeing to see" and my "ceremony in the weeds." This committed and purposeful preparatory work enabled the release of what I presumed to know and allowed me to find my feet again. It was deeply humbling work to develop a conscious resistance to my reflexive thinking so that I could be open to what might be revealed from a new paradigm within a context I am otherwise so deeply familiar with.

After years of developing invasive species education campaigns that vilified many weedy species, I needed a process to move myself away from this good plant/bad plant dichotomy. My purposeful process would involve a series of acts to get to know weeds in a way other than as targets for obliteration. I

commenced "A Ceremony in the Weeds" in the summer of 2017.
This is my ceremony.

*I recently went out collecting different "weeds" to dry for medicinal teas.
While healing teas have always been part of the traditional medicine I
practise, I mostly purchased them from the health food store. My daughter's
chronic illness sent me to the plants for help. I was desperate to find relief for
her, and the plants I knew I needed were weeds. Having never gathered these
plants for this purpose, I discovered an incredible mind block. While I knew
their medicinal benefits, I have also spent many hours advising others how to
kill and prevent the invasion of the very same plants. I had killed them
myself. The cognitive dissonance was hard to reconcile. I realized that I had
been successfully conditioned to view these plants negatively as enemies. I
realized that I prevented myself from getting to know these plants because it
is much easier to attack enemies you do not know.*

*The weedy medicines appeared between the raised garden beds of my
market garden and along the edge of the forest that surrounds our farm.
I had never really paid attention to them before, other than sending them an
annoyed glance as they represented yet another farmy task I needed to do.
Having given them pause for the first time, there I saw, illuminated by a ray
of sunshine like a light from the heavens, the bees pollinating them.* Damn.
*I looked away quickly as if caught staring at a stranger. I approached them
uncomfortably as I continued to watch at least three species of bees covered in
pollen upon them. Now what? Ordinarily when I collect plant medicines
I greet the plant, ask for permission to harvest, say a prayer of thanks, and
leave an offering. The very thought of doing that in this case felt strange.
Like it was far too personal of an exchange with my historic foes.*

*It felt silly but I thought perhaps I needed to introduce myself to them
first. It was awkward, and it did not feel like enough to overcome the
hurdle I felt. Then I apologized to the plants. "I'm sorry. I'm sorry*

I didn't see your potential before. I'm sorry I didn't give you and your relations more consideration." As weird as it sounds, it ended up being a humbling and deeply healing "conversation." I then asked the plants for permission to harvest them so that they could help my ailing daughter who, I went on to explain through tears, was suffering terribly. They said they would help. Through the blur of tears, I ceremoniously plucked horsetail and dandelion from the ground and picked the leaves of plantain and comfrey. Never had I been so careful with these yield reducers, indicators of poor soil health, and enemies of biodiversity. I now provide nurturing places for these pain relievers, infection preventers, and anti-inflammatories. When I find myself quick to judge, I think about those plants who helped me heal my daughter.

―――――――――

My eight-year-old son and nine-year-old daughters came outside to help me to collect my old enemies to include in our dinner. They thought the fact that we would actually eat weeds for dinner was hilarious. "Mom, have you gone crazy?!" asked Josh. Then we laughed and laughed at the ridiculousness of what we were doing. It was like some sort of weedy family betrayal. The experience made me realize that I had managed to successfully indoctrinate my own children with this anti-weed bias from an early age. Was that successful education on biological invaders or was I robbing them of their culture and the opportunities presented by these plants?

Dandelion pesto has become a family staple. It's confusing.

―――――――――

I have been working on the management of knotweed species across British Columbia for almost twenty years now. Knotweed I believe to be the weedy species that may deserve all the vilification I have hurled at it over the years. Destroyer of salmon spawning grounds, disrupter of riparian areas, destroyer of infrastructure, it is remarkable both in its ability to persist and in its ability to wreak havoc.

In 2014, I was diagnosed with Lyme disease. After a year of bizarre symptoms that eventually led to an inability to walk, an episode of Bell's palsy (partial facial paralysis), and forgetting where I lived, I finally got the diagnosis. Treatment was brutal. Multiple antibiotics at the same time. Terrible reactions to the bacteria dying off in my system. And to top it all off, an issue with C. difficile, which limited my antibiotic options.

I was much better at this point but not quite there, so my doctor gave me a couple of natural options to consider that had shown promise in studies against the Borrelia bacteria. She left the exam room and came back with a small glass bottle that had "Fallopia japonica extract" written on it. Thankfully my doc and I have a great relationship because I immediately blurted out, "You gotta be fucking kidding me!" She said, "What?!" I said, "You know what I do for a living, right?" and I pulled up a recent news piece about knotweed I had done on Global TV national news. She watched and began laughing hysterically. The very plant I was on the war path against—the plant I had killed hectares of and discussed in multiple news broadcasts—was the next line of treatment for my disease.

I wish I could say that I embraced this weed as part of my ceremony but I just couldn't bring myself to do it. I bought the bottle of the extract and it is still, years later, in my cupboard. At the time it was "knot" the treatment for me. I worried that the battle in my mind would have an impact on my ability to get well. Ultimately, I went with different plant medicine that could help resolve my symptoms. The scenario did offer me an interesting opportunity for a lesson about the potential of this plant for healing. Prior to this, I had watched YouTube videos of a guy promoting its medicinal benefits, but I had written the hippie and his *claims off. He was a bit of a pebble in my shoe as he widely promoted the medicinal benefits of knotweed and was critical of those of us working hard to kill it; his views posed a threat to our alien-plant-busting mission. While I still do not agree with his "live and let live" plant philosophy, I am at least receptive now to his message of knotweed's powerful medicinal benefits.*

I confess, we have Himalayan blackberry on our property. I made myself stop fighting it at two sites on our farm. Anyone visiting our property who knows me finds this strange. The thorny beast that started it all, the catalyst of my waging war on invasive species, allowed to live on my farm all these years later.

It had been driving me crazy to watch the blackberry expand in our yard. My commitment to this "unseeing" process made me leave it. I watched it. I considered it. I hated it. I admired it. I was grateful for it. Then I hated it again. One wouldn't think blackberry could cause such an emotional roller coaster, but for someone who passionately spreads the word, not the weeds, this process felt sacrilegious.

Then the bees arrived. I never realized how much the honeybees and our many native pollinators used this plant. With the declining populations of pollinators likely as a result of climate change and lack of availability of food, it made me wonder if the bees needed the blackberry. I assigned myself the task of looking for other pollen sources in our area, and the majority were domestic flowers. Squashes, tomatoes, cucumbers, fruit trees, lavender, mint, cilantro, peppers.

Then the berries arrived. My kids enthusiastically got their containers and wanted to go picking after dinner one evening. I grudgingly went along with this. I have long claimed my distaste for the blackberry out of principle. Applying food values to weeds can then make it difficult to have social licence from the public to kill them as part of invasive species management programs. I broke my rule and I ate some for the sake of science. The kids' happy, berry-stained faces made it palatable.

Then the bear came. We were doing dishes and cooking breakfast one morning and a young bear came sauntering past the kitchen window. He plotted a trajectory to the blackberry patch at the front of the property. Apparently, he didn't care that they are an invasive species. He was hungry, and with all the development nearby that has destroyed his habitat, I felt I had done something right by keeping the berry patch.

I confess that considering the blackberry has resulted in things becoming a lot less black and white. I tore up my arms as I pruned the thorny beasts back enough that they won't take over, but they can stay.

I bought weed seeds. Those seed sharers lurking at Seedy Saturdays— annual end-of-winter events in many towns where gardeners and farmers flock to buy and trade seeds—the ones I have shamed in the past for spreading invasive plants, I sought them out. Not to preach at them from my ecologically superior soapbox, either. I chose a vendor who would not recognize me, and I admired their extensive collection of all things weedy and invasive. I chose a few packets of seeds and gave them my money. I happily received their growing advice, having never attempted to deliberately cultivate these plants before. I shoved the seeds deep into my purse and kept my head down as I exited so I could pass my colleague at the Invasive Species Council booth undetected. When I got home, I planted the weed seeds in trays filled with our carefully crafted blend of soil in our greenhouse alongside our trays full of veggie starts. I am nurturing them alongside each other. It's weird.

My weedy colleagues think I've lost my damn mind.

———————

I tried to let go of control of the weeds on our farm. It was an incredibly busy summer—I had decided to try my hand at politics and entered the race to be a Member of Parliament in our federal government. With all the pressures that came with that, I just could not tend to the farm the way I normally could. As I sat in the middle of the garden early on in the campaign, looking around at the sea of weeds, I cried. I was completely overwhelmed. I realized I had to be okay with whatever happened. I simply had to let this go. Just for this year. So, I did. As the campaign wore on, the weeds kept on coming. I would look out over the garden from behind my laptop screen and see the weed seeds flying on the summer breeze. It should've been something peaceful to watch, but I knew they were simply planting themselves elsewhere. I would allow myself a moment of stress and then let it go. There is a lesson in the weeds, I would remind myself. A lesson about letting go. Not controlling everything in my life.

This is the part of the ceremony that is not such a fairy tale. If you are a weed scientist, or any kind of plant-savvy person, you know that there are consequences for simply letting things go. I watched as garden beds were overwhelmed by weeds. I watched the productivity of our crops go down. I saw how the beds dried out faster. I did watch some pollinators enjoy them. I watched my chickens eat some. Ultimately, the lesson of this ceremony in the weeds was that sometimes the information that you have from one way of seeing should be sufficient to inform your approach. For me, as someone who studies weed seeds, I knew what would happen. Letting go only meant more work for me in the subsequent years.

One year later, I am paying the price for "letting go." I am still busy. The solution was to stop the weeds before they appeared. Hire some help. Perhaps the silver lining is that I got to watch a lot of the processes I teach about first-hand, and I learned something about balance. As

I challenge myself to see things differently, I cannot simply throw out everything else I know. I cannot disregard the Western scientific knowledge keeper part of myself. That knowledge keeper is valuable. This is about knowing when to change lenses. This is about remembering to value all types of knowledges and developing the wisdom to know when to draw from each of them. It brought to light that developing that wisdom would be something requiring dedicated practice. Another ceremony perhaps.

I never really paid much attention to butterflies and pollinators before. Not until we moved from an agricultural region where they seemed to be plentiful (and we clearly took that for granted) to the rock of an island where we would start our new farmstead. Our property had the colonial shine of mostly rolling hills of neatly cut lawns and wood-chipped borders containing wheat-like, decorative grasses that dance when the wind blows. Not my cup of tea. My vision was different from the previous owners'. One that involved growing every possible vegetable, a greenhouse, chickens, and an orchard.

The first year we planted some apple trees along with the two that existed previously. That spring they flowered in glorious fashion and no pollinators could be seen on the abundant flowers. Nothing. I had never seen this before. I began to watch the skies for insects generally, and while the abundance of dragonflies in the summer delighted me, the lack of pollinators—and, for that matter, butterflies—was noticeable.

I began reading in earnest about which flowering plants would attract them, not only in pursuit of successful fruit production, but because by now the plight of pollinators and monarch butterflies had become mainstream news. The notoriety of this plight resulted in the endless production of seed mixes by seed companies all meant to entice them to the home garden. I would wander the seed sections of our local feed and gardening stores, reading the descriptive labels of the package contents, only to find non-native and invasive plants listed. Shaking my head at this lack of responsibility by the seed companies, and perhaps having a soft chuckle that they were keeping me gainfully employed (undoubtedly, I would be managing those invasive species that would eventually escape those gardens), I could not find what I believed to be a responsible solution to providing food for the bees and butterflies.

A perennial plant nursery had started up not far from our place, so I headed there. I was grateful for the knowledge of the nursery owner. Over the course of a few years, we continued to buy more and more perennial flowering plants (including non-native species) and began to have incredibly successful fruit harvests. Hundreds of pounds of apples and pears, all because we fed the bees. Our farm had come alive with the comings and goings and buzzings of more species of pollinators than I could count on both hands. I had dreamed of being able to have a farm that promoted biodiversity and here we were. One thing was missing, though. The butterflies.

We would have the occasional swallowtail come to visit, but the monarchs were nowhere to be seen. I began reading more in earnest about what was happening with their populations and, with the bee situation rectified, began purchasing more plants targeting the monarchs specifically. Another year went by; not a single one.

I went back to the perennial plant nursery, sharing my futile attempts with the owner. Knowing what I did for a living, she apologetically led me over to the butterfly bushes, Buddleia davidii. *We stood in silence in front of them. I know she was waiting for my immediate rejection of this quiet suggestion. For many years, I have spent countless hot and sweaty hours in the summer sun attempting to cut and dig out these bushes on the invasive plant list in parks and along roadsides. What she*

didn't know was that I was in the middle of my ceremony in the weeds.
She also didn't know that for all the hours I'd spent battling this plant,
I had always wondered why on earth we were getting rid of them. In
addition to observing countless butterflies and bees on them, they didn't
seem to be dominating any landscapes other than steep, hot ledges where
not much else grew. In my entire career, I had never come across a field
infested with butterfly bush. The worst I had seen was on gravel pit
edges. Doing what harm, I wasn't sure.

I didn't say anything. I went and got a wagon, loaded it with six pots
of butterfly bushes, and paid for them. We exchanged amused smiles as I
loaded them into my van. Off I went, carting invasive species that I had
just paid more money for than I care to disclose. When I got home, I
unloaded them and placed each of them in its pot in gaps along our
pollinator garden rock wall, which runs around forty metres long and
divides our yard from the fenced vegetable gardens. I brought my planting
shovel out and I couldn't bring myself to plant them. I put my shovel
back and left them in their pots, and continued to leave them all summer,
knowing full well they were not getting the water they needed from the
irrigation lines below their pots. I didn't want to feel bad about sort of
punishing them for being invasive and putting me in this situation, but
I did. As I felt these pangs of needing to save them, they began to flower
in their pots. The bees clearly loved them. So that was that. I dug the
holes, placed them in there, and rather than wishing them well, as I
usually do for everything I plant, I expressed more of a prayer of
forgiveness for what I may be inflicting upon our surrounding ecosystem.

That next year, those plants grew immensely. Of course they have,
I thought. They're invasive. It's what they do. I forced myself to weed
around them, trim them, and care for them like any other plant in the
pollinator garden. Occasionally I would catch myself admiring their
silvery leaves in the breeze and their cascading shape. Almost like a

fountain growing out of the earth. Then their cone-shaped flowers appeared in beautiful purple and pink shades. I continued to look for evidence of them spreading, but nothing. They really were beautiful. I noticed they were helping to provide shade for the plants growing around them. Giving them a break from the heat of the day. As I weeded, I observed that along with this shade came more moisture retained in the soil. Saving precious groundwater at a time when we worried about our well. With each redeeming feature I admitted to myself came a reluctant sigh. A continued wall I put up between me and these invasive plants I had willingly planted on my farm.

Until the day I'll never forget.

I was sitting on the deck writing a chapter for this book when something caught my eye. Fluttering. I saw a flash of yellowish orange and immediately told myself not to get too excited. It was probably a swallowtail. I can't help but think that the butterfly heard my inner thoughts as it flew right up to the deck, landing briefly on the railing, as if to show itself to me. Then it flew across the yard, narrowly escaping the hop of a curious chicken, and landed on one of the flowers of a butterfly bush. It was as though the whole thing was perfectly orchestrated. It was then that the flutters of two more on the other butterfly bushes caught my eye. Two years after bringing those plants home, finally, the monarch butterflies were here. I cried. It has been almost a month now since that day. And as I stood in the garden last night watering, I watched the comings and goings of monarch butterflies and all I felt for those butterfly bushes was gratitude.

My ceremony in the weeds has continued beyond my initial research journey. I realized through this transformative process that this was part of what it is to work from an Indigenous worldview. To always be seeking deeper connection to land and to all our relations. This practice is where wisdom is built. A knowing of place so intimate that any changes would be immediately apparent. A daily practice of place. Therefore, the simple use of Indigenous knowledge by those disconnected from place doesn't work. This ceremony helped me recognize that expertise is vulnerable to becoming a fast track to disconnection. An abandonment of the practice of acquiring wisdom. Our journey around the medicine wheel is not simply to go around once. It is a continuous cycle of renewal throughout our life's journey that deepens our relationality.

For me, this time in the eastern direction, this preparatory work, was an unexpected gift. It gave me a stronger connection with my culture, embracing plant medicine and empowering others to practise it too. I have deepened my relationship with the land such that I can now see the multitude of relationships with it and within it. It is as though I switched camera lenses from the laser-like focus of micro to something even bigger than the widest of wide angles. The psychological barrier of belongingness, of good plants/bad plants, is gone. My daughter is healed, and the weeds helped do that. The freedom gained by immersing myself in my ceremony in the weeds has not landed me in the professional crisis I thought it would. Instead, my colleagues have come alongside me, looking to go on their own journeys of making the old new again, working toward a "prepared beginner's mindset" to find new paths of inquiry that we need in this time of ecological crisis.

I was ready. And I was surprised to find I was not alone.

Part Three

Preparing for Change in the South

WE FIND ourselves ready for the rapid growth and transformation that come with the teachings of the southern direction of the medicine wheel. It is time to leap with humility and with faith that learning and applying these new-old ways will give us what we need to prepare for a hopeful future.

7.

Finding Ecological Balance with the Language of the Land Healers

EVERY YEAR, like most gardeners, I sit with hope at the end of winter and plan my garden. After spending the fall tending to the soils as we put the garden to bed for the winter, we have done the important preparatory work that gives us the promise of exciting possibilities for the coming season's harvest. I sketch an outline of the garden, its raised beds, the other growing areas we have established, and perhaps add in a new spot where we can squeeze in just a few more plants. To me, it is the most beautiful of blank canvases. To glance at it is to taste the crunch of a fresh cucumber, to smell the scent of basil, and hear the songs of the birds in the trees around it. While the canvas appears essentially blank, a mere outline, there is so much about the garden that I know with a careful intimacy reserved for very few other relationships in my life.

Over the years of nurturing plants in my garden, I have watched for where the sun hits each part of it throughout the growing season. I know which beds have the highest soil temperatures and which provide a reprieve from the intensity of the summer sun. I also know which beds the bunnies, who will inevitably breach my multiple attempts to fence them out, will munch on first. I have learned how to lengthen the growing season enough to get two full cycles in each year. I know which plant relations like certain places, who their friends are, and when to plant and ultimately collect their seeds. I even remember their lineages as I plant each successive generation to honour their connection to this place I also call home. I have gotten to know which seeds start best from the soil I have been working for years to create, and those who appreciate getting started from the safety of warm trays of potting mix in the greenhouse. I am aware of who is most vulnerable to the slugs missed by the chickens who enjoy their turn in the garden before we plant. I have seen what a difference it makes to give the chickens time there, scratching and mixing soils and eating insects. I know which weed species have shown up in the different growing areas and which pop up in between the beds. I think about the weed prevention strategies I will use based on my knowledge of the weeds' seed bank dynamics, life cycles, and reproduction and persistence strategies. I think about the pollinators that visit us each year and what food they need all season long. I know what my kids enjoy eating and which of the vegetables and fruits can be preserved in various ways to give us tastes of summer come winter.

Every year, I challenge myself to try to grow a new plant I haven't grown before. I also try new combinations of plants together and new growing methods meant to increase density to get the most out of the space we have. I reflect on the failures of the past. Those that came from certain seed sources, or problems with irrigation systems, or species that just didn't seem to like to call our farm home. I reflect on the successes. Plants that flourish, or offer unusual culinary opportunities, or don't require much help to do well. I consider the year ahead. What we have planned as a family, my professional ambitions, work-life balance. How much time I have to tend to the plants in my garden. I think about the patterns of the weather, especially the increased periods of drought and the consequences of extreme events like the heat dome.

With all that in mind and my favourite seed catalogues in hand, I begin to fill in the canvas, always starting with the simple plants. The cast of characters I know that everyone enjoys and that will do well. I place them carefully, thinking about where they lived last year, and finding them a new location that they would like for this year. I skim the catalogues for new varieties, sometimes prioritizing nutritive value, sometimes choosing plants just because they look beautiful. The aesthetic, an important consideration for my canvas. I think about the emotions I want to feel when I walk into the garden throughout the growing season.

This year's new challenge was establishing a cut flower garden. I used to think it a waste of time to grow things that one couldn't eat. Not worth the sacrifice of space unless they assisted with pest control. My newly gained affection for the variety and beauty that could be found in dahlias helped to overcome this bias. The challenge would be to grow purely for the joy of it, incentivized by the promise of beautiful flower arrangements on my kitchen table and in my office.

The canvas begins to take shape. All that is left is to fill in some of the gaps. I skim the pages of the seed catalogues once more and consult one last time with my family about what they like to eat from the garden. Any small remaining gaps are filled in with treats for the parrots and chickens and medicinal plants for making salves and soap. When finished, I take a wider lens to absorb what I have created in front of me. As I take it in, I have feelings that are difficult to fully articulate. A sense of hope and promise in keeping the bellies of my family full and in the life that will return with certainty to a place currently at rest. A sense of satisfaction that all the work, even in the seasons where we are not taking something from it, is well worth it. The anticipation that makes the winter pass more quickly, and the promise of a new growing season providing new lessons and new food.

I wonder if a painter feels the way I do as they plan and see their work come to fruition. There is so much that goes into a piece of artwork: the inspiration, the technical and artistic skill-sets, the care, collaborations. People always tell me that I'm a good gardener, usually attributing that to my education in agro-ecology. They admire the abundance and creativity in my garden without knowing all of what went into the creation of that canvas. Lessons and decision-making far beyond the singular lens of my Western scientific education. I know amazing artists and gardeners who didn't go to school in the conventional sense. Don't we admire their works regardless of any of that?

So often, the true experts of anything (whom I have met) have the most interesting and compelling personal stories that have influenced their journeys toward mastery, which only add to and deepen my appreciation and understanding of their creations. To me, it is so much like the ecological knowledge shared with me by our Elders and knowledge keepers. It is not coded in the language of science or presented as an assemblage of facts. Just like knowing different painting techniques doesn't make you an artist, knowing facts about ecosystems doesn't strengthen your connection to the land. The teachings of Elders offer wisdom and a deep understanding of place. These are the gatherers of many teachings from many sources who, over time and through depth of experience, know how they should be woven together and communicated in specific contexts. For Indigenous People, the knowledge is never separate from the wise ones.

When I reflect upon my garden canvas, I cannot help but marvel at all that goes into its creation. Responding to the needs of my family, my values, the connection I have had with plants since I was a barefoot toddler in my grandma's garden, my education in plant science, my years working with plants in the field and in my garden, the people I know from many walks of life and the knowledge they share with me, my own intuition, and anticipating weather patterns, pests, and diseases. All of it drawing upon the many dimensions of who I am. Not one more important than any other. I realize that my affinity for gardening is rooted in the challenge of developing the wisdom to process all those knowledges and balance all the considerations in the name of providing for the relations to be nourished by it. In many ways, gardening is my internship for young Eldership. Learning on the land, from the land, just as we are supposed to.

What, really, is the difference between a food grower like a gardener or a farmer and an ecologist? Perhaps these distinctions only continue to perpetuate the denigration of land-based knowledges and disregard the needs of our relations. Perhaps this distinction in the modern context is inhibiting us from doing the work we really need to be doing to bring healing balance to our lands and the relations upon them, humans included. These distinctions are keeping Eden ecologists from the pursuit of wisdom in the name of science. Perhaps the work of gardeners and farmers is essential training to build the wisdom to be an ecologist practising an Indigenous ecology.

Next year, I might try growing oats instead of quinoa.

Humans

Bringers of Balance

Shapers of the land and waters

When I use the terms *balance* or *balancer* to describe the role of humans in ecosystems, it is important to recognize that this is not the type of balance that has been debated over the history of ecology, which tends to be synonymous with *equilibrium*. *Balance* in the context of this work is a somewhat failed attempt to anglicize that which is an expressed sentiment of an Indigenous understanding of our role with our Earth. It is not something that required objectification within our own languages as it is the very pulse of our existence. Balance in this case is not a static condition; it acknowledges and accepts the dynamic nature of our ecosystems. It honours the past, present, and future. It recognizes and accepts that we cannot fully comprehend the complex number of and nature of the relationships within our ecosystems. It does not profess control over those systems. Instead, it puts forward a sentiment of responsibility to shape ecosystems into ways of being that meet the needs of our relations (animals, insects, fish, humans) and are consistent with community values. In essence, our role as balancers of ecosystems is a humbly accepted leadership role given to us by Creator.

The concept of balance in ecology has been debated throughout its history in scientific study. At the turn of the nineteenth century, American ecologist F. E. Clements had proposed a dynamic ecology which replaced the previous static descriptive work before him.[42] Then came ideas of equilibrium and stability, the "classical" or "equilibrium" paradigm, which persisted until the 1970s.[43] This paradigm fed the idea, in conservation and in the wider environmental movement, that there was a "balance in nature," easily upset by inappropriate human action. That equilibrium is naturalized as a "pre-disturbance" state—that is, the state of balance that existed prior to the disturbance of human activity.[44]

Fear not. Enter the ecologist. A hero cast by the conservation movement, who would, "external to natural processes, spanner in hand . . . put the balance right" when human action upset the machine.[45] As W. M. Adams puts it, "the scientific ideas and practices of conservation of this time were concerned precisely with establishing or recovering control, both over human impacts on nature (in stopping habitat loss) and over nature itself (in habitat management)."[46] While this was a role that recognized human responsibility to ecosystems, it differs entirely from the role of humans in the ecosystem in an Indigenous worldview. The ecologist is placed in a godlike position, above the ecosystem as external master fixer, the engineer of nature.[47] An Indigenous worldview, on the other hand, casts us as an equal part of the ecosystem; a leader meant to shape the system over time according to the values and needs of the ecological communities. This was not a single person's role to fulfill; the human community simply, as Elder Luschiim put it, "lived it."

Meanwhile, we exist in an ecology that is run by those who do not "live it" and yet we yield to their "expertise." Ecological restoration has taken scientific understanding to create rules for ecological restoration such that it can be executed in a cookie-cutter fashion.

If we are to allow an Indigenous ecology to take root once more, we must ensure that we can work together to create our collective garden. This comes in sharing a relational language. One that puts relationship in focus. One that ensures we are accountable for every decision made. One that centres our values and community needs. One that values wisdom. At this critical juncture it is as though, to me, we are all standing in front of a canvas with a mission to create a vision for the future that heals the planet. If we are to all pick up a paintbrush, we need to be able to communicate. If we want the art to look different from the status quo, we cannot work from the same old palette using the same old techniques we used before.

I have been told by Kwakwaka'wakw and Coast Salish friends that there was once a distinct language on the waters of the Salish Sea: the language of the fishermen. Fishing and managing the resource required the collaborative and cooperative efforts of those coming together on the water with their distinct languages and cultural identities. It was here where, when possible, political differences were set aside. Communication was key and a unique language was created to accomplish that. When I learned of this, I could not help but wonder, What about a common language for those caring for and stewarding lands?

This question resonated in my mind as I sat with Elders trying to figure out how to apply an Indigenous ecology. After they shared knowledge with me about some plants and how some important medicines seemed to be disappearing from certain areas, I said, "Well, what do we do?" I waited for their answer, but instead I was met with an uncomfortable silence, then a shared expression of,

"You are here to tell us." It is important to understand the significance of this. I have been taught that with Elders, I best listen and not talk much. I had been told before that it wasn't up to Elders to tell me what to do. They were there simply to share what they knew. Here I was again, holding knowledges and being reminded it's up to my generation to determine what to do with them.

Sitting in a new-found and scary leadership role among my Elders, I reflected that we had known of the declining populations of these medicines for a long time. Typical assumptions were made about what was causing this and actions were taken based on those assumptions. Assumptions and actions that were confined by the language of modern ecology and that, despite years of efforts, did not appear to be saving these medicines. Scientific language was keeping us from what we needed. The question of how we move forward applying a relational, Indigenous worldview to ecology suddenly seemed less daunting. A relational terminology would help us to move forward. The language of the land stewards. So began a deep dive into modern Eden ecological terminology and more meaningful discussion with Elders, knowledge keepers, and many of my colleagues whose work included restoration to begin the reclamation of having a distinct language for such an important responsibility.

The canvas of a modern Eden ecology is called an "ecological restoration plan." A term for what is often used to direct ecological restoration projects, and one which I had never given a second thought to. Until now. Their common format and contents are a dead giveaway of how far they are from the canvas of an Indigenous ecology. These plans will describe the target area geographically and perhaps describe the reason that the area to be restored was degraded. Many have generalized stated goals such as "restoration of the natural environment," "removal of invasive species," and planting "native species." These are well-intentioned documents and I have helped to write many of them. However, having now committed to a relational lens, when considering these plans I am taken aback by just how impersonal they are. Frankly, I am embarrassed to have participated in their creation. At the same time, I know that my friends and colleagues and I engaged in this kind of work with the best of intentions. We did not realize that the prescriptive and yet unspecific nature of these plans and the language used within them were largely incongruent with their intent to bring healing to the land.

Most of these plans made no mention of Indigenous knowledge up until more recent years. If they did, they certainly made no mention of a relational worldview, the very foundation of our knowledges. There was often no mention of the history of the land, or the origins of the very systems targeted for remediation. Where Indigenous communities were mentioned, it would only be as a stakeholder. Most of these documents lack specificity in their statement of goals. It is apparent now why we have strayed so far from truly being effective in healing the land—the more we have leaned on natural and applied sciences to substantiate ecology as a field of study, the further we are from the artful balance of an Indigenous ecology. The efforts of legitimizing an inherently relational practice using Western notions of science created terminology that fulfills its purpose in maintaining the facade of objectivity. We keep expecting a different result using the same language.

We are all different. We have different histories. Different families. Different experiences. Different support networks. Different roles to play. So do the trees. So do the fish. So do the birds. So do the plants.

The power of language is not to be underestimated. Simple changes in our language can completely change our perceptions, our ways of thinking and knowing, and our actions. A new language will help us to consciously transition toward an Indigenous ecology. It will provide the freedom we need to shift into the relational worldview.

I thought it would be difficult to depart from the language of modern Eden ecology. It is the very language I have used to describe and conduct my own work; it's also the language I used when communicating and promoting environmental awareness initiatives to the public and government. But I was wrong—the transition felt easy for me. Liberating, in fact.

What is it about this change in terminology that makes such a difference? The language of the application of modern Eden ecology is transactional and the language of an Indigenous ecology is reciprocal. Simply put, Eden ecology is business and Indigenous ecology is personal.

Many unhealthy relationships could be described as transactional, and these kinds of relationships allow for short-term exchanges. In ecological restoration, we often find "this for that" guiding our work instead of finding a path that honours our mutual dependence. Such transactional relationships make inequities possible; the characteristics of these relationships are not congruent with the spirit of ecological stewardship, yet somehow we find ourselves operating in this way and accepting it as our reality. It is evident in our language, approaches, compromises, and funding models. I believe that by consciously moving away from transactional language, we will quickly find ourselves resting upon the relational foundation of an Indigenous ecology, and at last realize the consistent, long-term successes we have been longing for.

To develop terminology that will help us to apply an Indigenous ecology, I consulted friends and colleagues involved in ecological restoration; this included staff at environmental nonprofit organizations, academics involved in various aspects of the field, and government staff (Indigenous and other). They were open to my ideas and shared their own. This collaboration, along with my review of ecological restoration plans from across North America, resulted in a list of commonly used terms from modern ecology. From this list, we identified and discussed the words that reflected transactional relationships, and those that presented the greatest opportunity to shift worldviews by replacing them with relational terminology. This exercise was not intended to change the entirety of commonly used vocabulary of ecological restoration—it was about finding those words or phrases that would provide a new circle of understanding. The beginning of developing a new language where people from all walks can come together united by values and work to bring healing to our lands.

This list is simply a beginning. I don't assert it to be *the* way but simply a start that I hope shows that words matter and have transformative power. I am asking you to be part of the creation of this language as part of our journey around the medicine wheel together, and consider how we might live an Indigenous ecology. Let us be reminded of its principles.

An Indigenous ecology:

- Rests upon a foundation of relationality.
- Is accountable to all relations.
- Is dependent upon humans fulfilling their role and responsibilities as balancers of the ecosystem.
- Embraces all relations equally.

- Is based upon reciprocity.
- Is focused on relationships.
- Does not objectify our relations.
- Is free from categorization, labelling, and dichotomies.
- Is respectful of all worldviews and their knowledges.
- Acknowledges the history of relationships with land and relations.
- Accepts all forms of knowledge acquisition.
- Embraces uncertainty.
- Adapts as it needs to whether it be over time or within a specific context.
- Is pragmatic.

Restoration is defined by the *Canadian Oxford Dictionary* as "the act of returning something to a former owner, place, or condition."[48] Stephanie Mills defined it as "the art and science of repairing damaged ecosystems to the greatest possible degree of historical authenticity."[49] This definition refers to damage caused by some sort of disturbance, such as development, pollution, deforestation, and perhaps an often-forgotten reason: loss of human relationship. It mentions repair according to historical authenticity, but, At what point in time? and Whose version of history? For me, this calls into question whether *restoration* is the right term for what we are trying to do.

Restoration implies that we are putting something back to the way it was. It was often the stated goal on many of the funding applications I wrote in my work with environmental nonprofit organizations. Having embraced Indigenous ecology now, I can see that "restoration" stated as a goal is too general, speaking only to the intention of the work. An intention that fails to acknowledge both the dynamic nature of our planet and the legacy of the relationships my ancestors had with the land. The term *restoration* can limit the scope of our actions by its very definition, casting us solely in the role of fixers. It creates the context for work with goals based on aesthetic notions of a non-existent natural state. It allows us to forget ourselves, the human relations, in the ecological equation, and creates an impersonal dynamic, one only between fixer and project.

The definition of this Indigenous ecology that I feel summarizes all of what I have learned on my research journey around the medicine wheel is *Relationally guided healing of our lands, waters, and relations through intentional shaping of ecosystems by humans to bring a desired balance that meets the fluid needs of communities while respecting and honouring our mutual dependence through reciprocity.*

We need to replace *ecological restoration* with terminology that reflects this definition and is powerful enough to bring awareness to, and encourage the shift toward, Indigenous ecology. We need a term that can bridge our worldviews.

There are several definitions that can be found for the verb *to heal*. The *Merriam-Webster Dictionary* defines it as "to make sound or whole; to cause an undesirable condition to be overcome; the process in which a bad situation or painful emotion ends or improves; and finally, the process of becoming well again."[50] While the definitions of *to restore* and *to heal* may seem similar, there is a fundamental difference in their connotation. *To heal* does not imply an automatic intention to return something to a particular state. I see these definitions of *healing* as offering greater flexibility and scope, and, most importantly, offering a feeling of hope through caring actions. We are not limited by a predetermined notion to putting anything back the way it was. It allows us to respond to the needs of the relations of the day and determine the appropriate balance for the relation or place.

I began suggesting to friends working and volunteering in the field of ecological restoration to begin using the word *healing* in place of the word *restoration*. It has been a well-received change. A good friend of mine who has worked in the field for almost thirty years said, "It makes my work beautiful." I agree. The word *healing* immediately places us in relation with what we are doing. An act of kindness and caring as opposed to assuming the role of a fixer, like a mechanic. We are not doing something to an object, we are helping a relation or relations. It immediately transforms our work into the relational worldview, providing freedom in our intentions and placing a responsibility upon us as healers to consider who we may be trying to help. We are moved away from transactional relationships and into reciprocal relationships.

Relatedly, when referring to those doing the work of *land healing*, we should refer to them as *Land Healers* and *Water Healers*. We know them mostly as volunteers, stewards, stream keepers, and government employees. The people out there often in the pouring rain, freezing cold, trying to do the right thing for our planet. Using the term *Healer* commands respect. Healers in our Indigenous communities take care of physical and spiritual wellness. They are valued advisers in bringing healing of all types to a community. We need to offer the same respect to our Land and Water Healers that we often reserve for other types of healers in our lives such as doctors. For the many great Land Healers out there doing their best, I hope that you take this new term with great pride and are treated with the reverence you deserve as another crucial Healer of our communities.

There are different kinds of healing, including physical, spiritual, and cultural. Healing spans time and space. We can heal old wounds, we can heal newer wounds, and we can find healing as we evolve and flourish. We can find healing in creating promise for the future. Healing can be both specific and continuous. It can be a manner of tending to a specific harm or it can be nourishing a relationship. To use the word *healing* as in *land healing* or *water healing* allows us to move beyond the limits of objectifying the components of generalized transactions to embrace the boundless potential of relationality.

Our Indigenous ecology departs from the use of dichotomies. It does not vilify species through categorization processes with roots in colonialism. While there are many species that have been historically present within certain ecosystems that are important, we must remember the dynamic nature of both our ancestors and the planet. While we have already addressed the issues with the native versus non-native species dichotomy, it is important to acknowledge just how deep-seeded these terms are within the application of modern ecology. In particular, the presence of "native species" has become the gold standard measurement of success for ecological restoration. A change in terminology will help us to move away from this polarizing guidance in our land healing efforts.

As we work toward the desired ecological balance of a particular place, there will be species that we do and don't want and everything in between. In placing ecology upon a relational foundation, we must consider species in terms of their contribution toward the desired balance of a particular system. We do this by considering their relationships with other relations as opposed to assigning generally applied positive or negative labels to them.

This reminds me of what I was taught once in a parenting course—we should never label a child as good or bad. Instead, we assign an attribute to the action or behaviour they are exhibiting. For example, Billy's behaviour was bad. It describes the nature of the relationship between Billy and his action. Billy is not inherently bad. Billy is not a bad child. Perhaps Billy just has tendency to behave in certain ways in certain contexts. If we are to embrace our Indigenous ecology, we need to apply a similar approach when it comes to species evaluation.

If we consider species, it allows us to evaluate them with an open mind; to consider a plant's potential contributions and/or what changes they could bring to a specific system; to have open and difficult conversations about climate change and adaptation. This is about maintaining the epistemic openness of an Indigenous ecology. Thoughtful or sympathetic regard for our relations, wherever they may be from, honours them by focusing on their relationship potential and behaviours.

When we apply labels to certain relations, it is difficult to see them as anything different. It is that simple. If Himalayan blackberry is a "bad plant" and you find it in your yard, you are more likely to think, "I need to get rid of that bad plant." I have provided examples of plants that became part of the traditional medicines of many of our Indigenous communities. Many of these plants, even now, are considered "bad plants"—St. John's wort and burdock are examples. I don't deny that we had good reasons for controlling that blackberry to begin with. This is certainly consistent with the approach of Elders I have worked with on invasive species issues.

As a specialist in this field, I have found it frustrating that even considering the possible benefits of an invasive species is in some way undermining our field of study. We need the freedom to challenge assumptions as it opens up new pathways of scientific understanding. For example, now that we have greater understanding of mychorrhizal networks, the underground web of relationships between trees, plants, and fungi, could it be possible that there are so-called invasive species contributing to forest health? This notion was likely to be dismissed historically, but since more recent groundbreaking research, it is now a meaningful area of inquiry. Elder Luschiim said to me, "Well, why is that plant [as in an invasive species] there? What is it doing? What is it trying to tell us?" Good questions. Questions we've not been freely able to ask.

Perceived nativeness does not help us to reach the ecological "balance" we need either. "Native" species have become almost untouchable even when they need to be reduced for the benefit of other desirable relations. What is the definition of *native* as it pertains to plant species anyways? From what point in time of their recorded history in a place are they considered native enough?

If we are giving *relational consideration* to species in order to establish the desired balance, then we shall shift terminology to describe species as those that are *relationally preferred*. In some cases, we may not know much about the contribution of formerly vilified species, and thus this change of language may even catalyze research into their potential benefits to systems. Species vilification created the perception that research on them wasn't needed at all or, if they were researched, influenced the nature of research questions regarding those species. Such a departure could bring new and exciting findings. What learning have we now opened ourselves up to?

FROM *NATURAL AREAS* TO *LEGACY AREAS*

The problem of the assertion of naturalness was addressed earlier in the book. If we are truly working to heal the land, we must honour its true history and the deep relationship between it and the Indigenous people who have lived and still live there. We need to move away from this assertion of naturalness or a natural state. Period. Not just when we are discussing *land healing*. Instead, let us refer to these areas as they are and acknowledge them as *legacy areas* or the *legacy state* (of balance). The definition of *legacy* in the *Merriam-Webster Dictionary* is "something transmitted by or received from an ancestor or predecessor or from the past."[51] *Legacy areas* are a gift. One that may have been carefully tended to be some of what remains today. The term *legacy* to replace *natural* helps us to keep our connection with our relations, past, present, and future. The term is inherently relational as it spans space and time. We can honour the legacy of the past and work together to create our own legacy to pass on to our children. There is nothing accidental about that.

Asserting a natural state takes us out of the picture. It is highly offensive to Indigenous Peoples as it is a colonizing practice that permeates modern ecology. We must honour the purposeful relationships of Indigenous Peoples with their lands by acknowledging them. *Legacy state* makes sure we never forget, and that we work to honour them. There is great responsibility that goes with creating legacies, and this change in terminology ensures we remember that.

FROM *STAKEHOLDERS* TO *HUMAN RELATIONS/PARTNERS/BALANCERS*

The term *stakeholder* is frequently used when gathering relevant humans together who have a shared interest in a particular place that may be destined for land healing. It is more commonly used by government agencies to describe such gatherings and related processes; for example, in phrases like "consultation with stake-holders." The word has always made me cringe. I know many of my colleagues involved in caring for a place or waters have a similar response.

Stakeholders is a very impersonal term that transforms the land into a commodity, taking the personal relationship out of the process so that rational decisions can be made. It is sort of like the "It's not personal, it's business" of the land and water healing "business." Stakeholders can have unequal interests in a place, or be affected unequally by the impact of decisions that may be made. Categorizing the carers of our lands and waters as "stakeholders" makes room for inequity and places those with "stakes" at odds with each other. The terminology feels oppositional. Those who have stakes in an environmental issue (other than economic ones) often lose to those with the greatest economic stakes as this terminology passes the greatest power to them in determining outcomes.

We need a term that emits a sense of equality among all who gather with shared interest in a place; one that acknowledges the relationships that exist to the place to be healed. A preferred term that is already frequently used is *partners*. Another term that I have begun using when gathering interested people together to discuss land healing issues is *human relations*. While I know that some folks feel that is a bit strange, it is a concrete reminder of relationality and it unites us. As we apply an Indigenous ecology, addressing groups as a gathering of human relations brings a rev-erence to our responsibility in coming together as *balancers*. Regardless of what term is used to describe those assembling for the purposes of land healing, it must be a term that unites, equal-izes, and brings relationality to the forefront.

ADDITIONAL TERMINOLOGY AND SUGGESTED RELATIONAL SHIFTS

Following is a list of additional terms commonly used in ecological restoration with suggested replacement terms that are reflective of our Indigenous ecology. I have not provided additional explanations or justifications as overlapping themes will become repetitive. I have left some of these blank as they require further discussion and I hope provide an opportunity for your own contemplation. The purpose of this list is to demonstrate what more work needs to be done and the type of consideration we must give to how we have ordinarily completed land healing projects.

COMMON TERMINOLOGY OF ECOLOGICAL RESTORATION	SUGGESTED TERMINOLOGY FOR INDIGENOUS ECOLOGY
Ecosystem function	Ecological balance
Ecosystem health	State of desired ecological balance
Ecological disturbance	Ecological balance disruption or imbalance trigger
Restoration target	Desired ecological balance
Community dynamics	Relationships of relations
Ecological stability	Balance resilience
Species diversity	
Ecological integrity	
Biodiversity	
Management	Caring, stewarding, balancing
Conservation	

Common terms in ecological restoration and suggested replacement terms that would better reflect Indigenous ecology.

As I began to test the new terminology for an Indigenous ecology with my friends, colleagues, and other knowledge holders, I was overwhelmed with how openly it was embraced. A colleague said to me, "It's as if we finally have permission to use words to express what we were actually trying to do without the fear of seeming unscientific." Yes! This was my own experience as well. It was finally okay to use words that captured the very essence of this deeply personal work, transforming it to become deeper, actionable, and meaningful, without the illusion of scientific detachment. It immediately felt more effective and connected. As we piloted some of the newly proposed terminology in a land healing project meeting, for the first time in a long time I felt empowered instead of defeated.

It is time for a language of the land stewards. One that enables us all to fulfill our responsibilities to the land, embrace relationality, and act in reciprocity. One that allows us to sit and have the difficult, high-stakes discussions to bring healing to complex ecological systems and to be honest about the complex decisions to be made. A language that is rooted in reciprocity and humility and makes clear the specific intentions of land healing efforts. A language that makes it easier to talk about values and needs alongside a decolonized and Indigenized science. A language that can help researchers direct their work. A language that can attempt to address power asymmetries that come with colonial organization of land ownership while we have the grander conversation about #landback. A language that makes it impossible to make decisions for lands, waters, and resources without being on and intimately knowing those lands. A language that ensures that the right Peoples and relations are not missing from conversations that determine what happens to those lands, waters, and resources.

The ease with which we are able to decide who stays and who goes should be an immediate indicator—a warning even—that we are moving further away from an Indigenous ecology. Anything so complicated deserves the honour of time to ensure careful consideration.

At the heart of it, I believe that all who care for our Earth Mother in any respect are united by good intentions; however, modern ecology has just made it difficult for our good intentions to come to fruition. History has shown us that paradigm shifts can be difficult. The difference in this case is that the intentions of those from each worldview are not in opposition. We are united in our desire to bring healing to our land and waters. I believe our shared intentions and experiences where modern ecology has failed us (despite our best efforts) have brought us here together. We are all ready for something that will finally close this ever-widening gap between our intentions and the efficacy of their application. With this new language, the language of the land stewards, we make possible the profound transformation of ourselves from the "fixers" with the best technical information to the "balancers" guided by wisdom. Just as Creator wanted.

8.

Forest Gardens, Webwork, and Ecological Leadership

AT THIS point in our journey I'll share stories told by knowledge keepers, and I'll provide examples of legacies of human leadership of our ecosystems from pre-contact times that can be seen on our lands and in our waters today. Legacies that we chase today without an understanding of the purposeful shaping of lands and waters by Indigenous Peoples remain unattainable. These stories will remind us of the knowledge and power we hold and give us permission to reclaim our critical role in the health of our planet once more.

We'll begin with the Kwakwaka'wakw story, as told to me by Kwakwaka'wakw knowledge holder and fisherman Thomas Sewid, of how Creator created balance in the ecosystem by giving humans a leadership role.

THOMAS SEWID:

It is said that the Creator came to the world and created the air, land, mountains, trees, and waters. Throughout his creation, he placed animals of all sorts that we know of today as well as the supernatural animals that are no longer with us, such as Thunderbird. He left the world expecting that one day he would return and see that the animals lived in harmony and, in their harvest, that they kept balance within the animal kingdom.

Creator was wrong. Upon his return thousands of years later, he saw that the animal kingdom was all out of balance. There were regions where there were too many creatures eating salmon and salmon were not returning to spawn. The animals that relied upon salmon, young and old, were starving. In some cases, some species went extinct.

There were areas where there were too many hooved animals and they were eating or had eaten all the greenery. The wolves were now starving, and sickness spread through their ranks. Other animals in these regions had no grasses, shoots, buds, nuts, or seeds. They, in turn, were starving. Their species was becoming endangered or in some cases had disappeared altogether.

They say that there were so many wolf packs in some regions, they had eaten all the meat-bearing animals and they were now suffering; warfare erupted between the packs. It is even said that there were so many bears, the makers of trails in the forest, that their trails intertwined and created massive labyrinths. The bears became lost, and in their confusion they would cross paths and fight.

The whole animal kingdom was out of balance and Creator saw what he had done wrong. He had not created an animal to provide balance. So he decided that this animal he would create would be called human. The humans would harvest animals and plants for food and for social and ceremonial needs. The humans would be the mechanism to help keep balance in the animal kingdom, which would be maintained through their mutual reliance and respect. Creator, being out of magic, could not do this. He journeyed to the north end of the world where ice never melts. He landed and walked through the great doors of a Guk'dzi (Big House) made of ice. Inside he found his brother, the Transformer, sitting in a chair of ice.

He told his brother that he was out of magic and that it was up to the Transformer to help rectify the wrong the Creator had made. The Transformer was to journey through the world and transform animals he came across into the first humans. These first humans would keep their crest animal of origin as their family crest. They would find another human to marry, and they would have children. The humans would then harvest the plants and animals to feed themselves and their children. In doing so, they would help keep all animals in balance within the animal kingdom. This is how it was for thousands of years and we now know where the Kwakwa̲ka̲'wakw and other coastal Tribes come from and how our lands and waters were always kept in balance insofar as all the animals.

Humans. Balancers of the ecosystem. What an incredible responsibility this is. Understanding this may help settlers to understand what is at the very core of being an Indigenous person. Our very existence, as it was intended, essential to the health of all relations of the lands and waters on Turtle Island. After contact, everything changed—the loss of ecological balance a direct consequence of colonization. We were no longer free to fulfill our essential role, which was now determined by the settlers. Settlers described in their letters home the abundance of resources they found in the new world, when in fact what they observed was the bounty of purposefully shaped ecosystems. A balance maintained through our intimate relationship with our lands and waters and careful acts of reciprocity by us for our relations. A balance of mutual reliance for mutual flourishing. If only the settlers had realized that. As soon as the exploitation of this perceived abundance began, our Earth Mother was set on her current trajectory. Balance lost.

I refer to the ecological balance prior to and at the time of contact as the "legacy balance," as it is now a vestige of the time when we fulfilled our role as ecological balancers. We must understand the commitment and connection to our land and waters that was required for the legacy state to have existed. The more time that passes since Indigenous Peoples worked to purposefully shape ecosystems that supported specific species, in this case iconic coastal species, the harder it will be to influence the current states of these systems to sufficiently support them. We are experiencing the consequences now as we witness our salmon populations collapse and our southern resident killer whales starve here on the coast of the Salish Sea.

THOMAS SEWID:

People celebrate the increase in humpback whales to our waters in the Salish Sea these days. They say, "Isn't it amazing to see these wonderful animals in our waters?!" Same with all the sea lions. But I don't share that sentiment. It worries me. We have never seen so many here. Why are there so many and yet so few resident orcas? So few salmon? It is an indicator of change for me. It is a change in balance in the ecosystem. Not necessarily the change we want.

———

While ecosystem collapse is a complicated equation with many contributing factors, at the core of it is this very simple explanation: We collectively have ceased to fulfill our role as the balancers. If we continue only to address environmental degradation, we will continue to only treat the symptoms of the greater problem. We will work only within the confines of the current balance—or imbalance, depending on your perspective.

Perhaps this will help to make sense of how our current environmental reality is possible when we live in a time of great scientific knowledge, sophisticated technological innovation, and increased environmental awareness. It certainly made it clear to me why countless attempts at restoration projects I was involved with failed, especially over the long term. The current balance will not support all our relations that functioned within the legacy balance to which the settlers arrived and on which they imposed their resource economies. Economies that continue operating under the false assumption that this legacy state was both permanent, the default, and natural.

The colonial notion of who Indigenous Peoples were prior to contact, and who they are today for that matter, is a critical piece of the problem of bringing healing to our lands and waters. The hunter-gatherer perception seems a bit like a burr stuck to modern Eden ecology that we just can't quite get rid of. In fact, its continued influence makes me think of a burr once left for too long in my horse's mane, leading to more and more of a matted mess that got more and more difficult to fix the longer I left it. Eventually I had to shave off my mare's entire mane. So perhaps here we are, dispelling the hunter-gatherer myth, starting fresh before this burr causes any further harms. The good news is that what we need to do to shed this denigrating perception is not very complicated at all. It is a matter of basic numbers and basic history.

We need only to apply a food systems lens to our pre-contact ecosystems, and to understand pre-contact population sizes. The pre-contact population of Indigenous Peoples in what is known as British Columbia has estimates ranging from a conservative two hundred thousand to one million people. Narrowing our focus to the area I live in, a very conservative estimate of the pre-contact population in the coastal areas along the Salish Sea is approximately thirty thousand people. The stories told by ancestral village sites, through oral histories and archaeology actively being done today by many Indigenous communities, immediately dispel the hunter-gatherer myth, as many villages along the coast had more than one thousand people living in them with additional villages nearby. I tell people to think about what it takes to feed your own family. How much food do you need in a year? If you have a garden, how much of your annual food is coming from that garden? Now think about how much food your neighbourhood needs (think suburbia). Now imagine there are no grocery stores or infrastructure to support the movement of food from all over the world to you. Everything that you need comes from within a reasonable distance; for example, within your territory.

I should dispel another myth here about coastal and Interior Indigenous Peoples: we didn't just eat fish. We know from archaeological records, ethnoecological work completed by researchers such as Dr. Nancy J. Turner, and oral histories that diets were approximately 60 percent plant-based.[52] Given the numbers of people, and how much of that diet was plant-based, would it make sense to be scouring all over far-reaching lands for those plants? No. Of course not. Colonial agriculture has been used as a weapon against Indigenous Peoples on the very lands that were stolen from them. It continues to be asserted as the benchmark for settler superiority in terms of civility, sophistication, and proof of land ownership. *Agriculture* defined by the *Merriam-Webster Dictionary* is "the science, art, or practice of cultivating the soil, producing crops, and raising livestock and in varying degrees the preparation and marketing of the resulting products."[53]

Agriculture is merely a label used by settlers for food growing. When the settlers arrived on our shores and looked at the vast forest lands, they didn't see our food growing because it didn't look the same as their food growing. Our agriculture didn't require the clearing of vast sections of lands. What they saw was untamed wilderness and a magical abundance of resources. In fact, pollen records found in food-cooking hearths, soil signatures of intensive food growing, soil profiles indicating soil cultivation including amendments, obvious changes in plant communities that can be seen within forests today, and oral histories from numerous Indigenous communities—such as the Ts'msyen, Cowichan, Nuu-chah-nulth, and Haida—tell a completely different story.

Having stood in some of what are being referred to as "forest gardens"[54] and other Indigenous food-growing areas today, I must share that those experiences have been life changing. So often our oral histories are not believed or semi-believed with doubt cast upon them. And here, today, is overwhelming physical evidence that we in fact "farmed." The very weapon used against us to continue to keep our lands from us, neutralized by finding these legacy-state food-growing areas. I had heard from Elders about them, and possibly been in some that were severely degraded. I will never forget walking into the dense bush of the north coast without a trail, seeing a small opening in the canopy, and there, in the filtered sunlight, finding plant species that don't otherwise "belong" in the area, in densities and species composi-tions (mixes) that would never be expected within that forest type. All conveniently located alongside ancestral village sites that have been identified clear as day using newer remote sensing technologies such as LiDAR.

These lands were loved and actively cared for. Plants were bred, moved, planted, propagated, watered, fertilized, harvested, preserved, and stored. High-density production was required to feed that many people—of course it was. It is nonsensical to think that it wasn't, but that is the power of stories.

I will mention here that I do not like the term "garden" used in the context of Indigenous food-growing systems. To me it perpetuates the denigration of what were highly intensive, sophisticated systems meant to feed many people all year long. However, because they have been named as such within the context of research projects, I will refer to those projects using that term.

In our efforts to reclaim and revitalize forest gardens to make them once again part of Indigenous food systems, we confront some of the colonial notions of naturalness, forest management, and conservation head-on. All because Eden ecology does not recognize humans as leaders in our ecosystems. Human leader-ship is evident in traditional stewardship practices such as remov-ing trees to allow for the required light, using fire to "sweeten" the land (in the name of amending the soil to maximize berry production), propagating plants through cuttings, and fertilizing soils with fish bones, to name just a few. Decisions about who stays, who we want more of, and who goes. A leadership that requires accountability for those difficult decisions that must be made to ensure all are fed while walking gently on our lands.

Other important examples of Indigenous food growing along the coasts of the Salish Sea include aquaculture, so often perceived as something settlers brought to our coastlines. Clam gardens were established up and down our coasts.[55] Suitable areas found and manipulated to be able to produce shellfish such as clams and geoducks, more intensively than in a gathering fashion. Elders describe how new genetics, sometimes referred to as "fresh blood," from other areas were frequently introduced into these gardens to ensure clam health. Signs of these gardens can easily be seen along the coastline if you know what to look for. Further evidence upon the shorelines of these clam gardens are the middens full of shells from harvesting and processing. Fresh and dried clams were not only important for food security but also incredibly important to the coastal economy. Dried clams were coveted by my own Nlaka'pamux relatives in the Interior of the province, who traded for them.

This leadership of our waters to provide food extended into other fisheries. My friends farther north up the coast of Vancouver Island describe how they introduced pink salmon to streams where they did not live before as they wanted to "set the table" by having access to those fish without having to leave their territories. Fish traps can also be seen up and down our coasts—again, if you know what to look for. In front of our family cabin is a large tidal fish trap where rocks have been carefully stacked to create a wall in front of a pool. When the tide comes in (floods), the fish come into the area. As the tide goes out (ebbs), some fish get trapped inside the pool as the water drops below the level of the wall.

In addition to a food systems lens, we cannot forget to apply a technological lens to our ecosystems, as the lands and waters were shaped for these purposes as well. Specific tree stands were managed for different technological needs—for example, cedar was managed to make specific types of canoes, shingles, and boards. Very specific wood was needed for different uses. Some technologies needed knots, other knots were undesirable. Some cedar needed to grow as big as possible and straight to become giant war canoes, and so tree stands were managed to allow for that. What was made abundantly clear to me by knowledge keepers was that cedar is not simply cedar. The forests were managed specifically for what was needed, even within the same species.

Much more detailed accounts of these food-growing, food-getting, and technological systems can be found in other sources, some of which I have referred to in the Notes section of this book. My introduction of them to you here is to reveal what is so often unrecognized and, by remaining so, reinforces misperceptions about our people and leaves us locked in an ecology that will not heal our sickened planet.

While I watch the collapse of Pacific salmon, and I see the resources and efforts going into their recovery, I keep finding myself holding my head in frustration as no one seems to ask, What shaping of systems was required for their flourishing while meeting the needs of all relations reliant upon them? It's clear that we live in a very different world now, including a different climate, but we cannot disregard the legacy state as it is critical to informing our actions today. Did you know that children used to learn to hunt sitting on the banks of the mouths of rivers and creeks, targeting mergansers and other waterfowl? Birds that fill their bellies with salmon fry? We used to hunt seals and sea lions who now make their way up our rivers targeting salmon. We used to clean our fish and clams on the banks of the rivers and the ocean and bring them farther inland for processing. Reciprocity was part of our harvest.

There is much more responsibility in taking on the role of the balancer—responsibility for our relations, all inhabitants of Turtle Island, as we accept our role in the determination of their fate through purposeful action. We accept that we must be accountable to them. Both for how they have been harmed post-contact and now as we take back our role as the balancers. Our decisions will have an impact on all relations, and they will not necessarily be positive. In every situation, difficult choices lay ahead. There are two possibilities: We can choose to accept a new ecosystem balance, embrace different relations making new homes, and accept the consequences that our legacy relations (those relations who inhabited a specific area at the time of contact) may play a lesser role, move elsewhere, or disappear altogether. Or we can choose to attempt to regain the legacy ecological balance and hope that this is possible within our current context.

Whatever we decide, we must be prepared for the challenge of evaluating these options and work carefully as we determine the desired relational balance. Which relations stay? Which relations go? Who do we need? For us to make a meaningful difference, we must find ways to answer these difficult questions. Which relations can the current climate support? Who can the future climate support? What are our values?

It is one thing to say that we need to bring Western scientific knowledges and Indigenous knowledges together. It is quite another to answer the question of how we do this effectively as we make decisions about land and water healing and the management of our relations often known as natural resources. I have spent considerable time hearing the increasing calls for the inclusion of Indigenous knowledge into science, and those making compelling arguments about why this should be done. I have been left frustrated that these calls are not followed up with plans for how we go about achieving this.

It is still early days and we, Indigenous Peoples and our allies, are all trying to figure this out. We are trying and making mistakes along the way, but progress is there. If we are looking for a perfect recipe, then we are missing the point. Nothing about working together should ever be cookie-cutter. All the more reason it is important that we share our often iterative processes. If you are not a Land Healer, or ecologist, or researcher, this detailed "how" in my case may not seem necessary for your completion of our journey around the medicine wheel. However, I think any ally should want to learn about not just decolonizing a process, but Indigenizing one too. While you may not be planning large-scale land healing projects, you may be volunteering for a local stewardship organization, or you may be in a totally different career that is looking to lift Indigenous voices. There are lessons here for you too.

Earlier discussions about the nature of our relationships with our land and waters, and the need to shift to relational terminology, were all meant to lead and prepare us for this point in our journey. At last, we find ourselves sitting on the relational foundation of our Indigenous ecology. Seeing land healing anew. So now what? How do we make decisions as Land and Water Healers? How do we determine the desired balance? How do we establish the balance? How do we put into action the language of the land stewards?

My act of reciprocity for my research journey was to develop a framework for land management decision-making consistent with our Indigenous worldview and values for Cowichan Tribes. Like many of the intentions that I set out with at the beginning of that journey, this one also needed to change to reflect what I learned along the way. The term *framework* no longer felt appropriate. It became clear that such a structure was not congruent with guiding a process from a relational worldview such as the application of an Indigenous ecology.

Frameworks are ordinarily used to assist with guiding a process. A good framework provides a clear path to navigate complicated processes. Just as we needed to shift some of our ecological terminology to ensure we are working from a relational worldview, we need to shift the way we guide our decision-making processes. It is important that we not impose a colonial structure upon our use and application of an Indigenous worldview. For too long, Indigenous academics and knowledge holders have had to try to make our work fit into processes that are not designed to fully embrace it. The full benefit of our work cannot be realized if we allow it to continue to be compromised in this manner. It became clear to me that this act of reciprocity would have a dual purpose. Not only would we design a guiding process for the application of an Indigenous ecology, but we would also design a new guiding process for relational decision-making.

Love settles within the circle, embracing it and
thereby lasting forever, turning within itself.
Luther Standing Bear, Oglala Sioux

It seemed a natural choice that the application of an Indigenous worldview to science, in this case, Indigenous ecology, be guided by a process grounded in circular symbology. The circle is deeply significant to us. While there is variation in its use within different Nations and different communities, its foundational significance is similar. The circle symbolizes our connection to the cyclical nature of life. The lives of people, the seasons, the sun, the moon. It symbolizes the four directions and the elements (air, water, fire, earth). Circles symbolize harmony, balance, and peaceful interaction among all living beings.

The work of land and water healing should be guided by a process that not only is reflective of the relationality of the Indigenous worldview but also acknowledges the extensive and intricate nature of relationships we are attempting to balance. I have called this guiding process webwork. *Webwork* is not a noun to describe a guiding process, as *framework* is. As we embrace an Indigenous worldview, we embrace the nature of our Indigenous, verb-based languages. *Webwork* is a verb (or what I like to call an Indigenized noun) which describes relations being guided by the process of creating relational webs and weaving them together for the purpose of bringing healing. Each webwork process guides those coming together in circle who are linked by their shared values and intentions to create a path forward toward a desired balance.

Instead of explaining what webwork is and how it can be used in step-by-step fashion, I am going to share examples from the process of its development, which was born out of opportunities to introduce friends, students, and colleagues to an Indigenous worldview and its application to science—in this case, its use in land and water healing efforts. Encouraging others, especially well-seasoned professionals in a field of study, to shift worldviews can be very difficult. I figured out quickly that this process must begin with generating enthusiasm and interest at the prospect of what the opportunity offered. The keenness I was met with, which was completely surprising, made it less an attempted sell at the potential of something outside-the-box, and instead an exercise in bringing people alongside as collaborators.

Before bringing anyone into webwork, it is important to ensure that there is foundational understanding of the topic at hand. In this case, I worked hard to ensure that everyone coming into the circle was comfortable with what an Indigenous, relational worldview was, and with the principal concepts of Indigenous ecology. Whether I was beginning multi-stakeholder environmental meetings, or just talking one-on-one with a colleague, I began with exercises such as the "putting on glasses to see connections" example I used earlier in the book to help solidify understanding and increase comfort level with working relationally. Creating scenarios for visualization helped them practise seeing relationally. For example, having them imagine themselves somewhere outside where they often go. Perhaps where they walk their dog every day, or a favourite place to hike or fish. Somewhere so familiar that they feel they know it well. I would then ask them to put on their "relational glasses" and tell me what relationships they see in that place. The enthusiasm was infectious. One fun example was a friend who said, "Hey, there are the birds I see on the grass every morning. They are aerating it as they peck and scratch for food. Hey, that helps the grass! Oh, but those poor worms that become their breakfast!" How quickly we can see the relationships between all the relations through our imagination if given the opportunity. I asked most people who did this exercise what that experience was like, and many shared that the familiar location seemed like an entirely new place. This was exactly the goal. To show them how they can completely transform well-known surroundings by seeing through a different lens. Step one of webwork completed: unleash the power of relational thinking.

With the power of relational thinking unleashed, to gain comfort with Indigenous ecology I presented the language of the land stewards and provided opportunities to adopt new terminology, encouraging those participating to come up with their own substitutions. In a couple of cases participants pulled up one of their own existing ecological restoration plans, or policy, and we went through as they changed the wording to become consistent with Indigenous ecology. I'll say that many laughs were had through these processes as experimenting with new terminology is quite fun (there was certainly some entertainment value) and it offered an excellent example of the contrast between work done from the dominant paradigm and an Indigenous worldview. Suddenly it seemed wrong to call plants simply "weeds." Instead, options such as "opportunist of damaged ground relation," "preventer of soil erosion," "relation that will grow where no one else will," and "sole provider of food for pollinators" emerged. We changed terminology to describe projects from "enhancement" to "fortification," and from "environmental assessment" to "consideration of land relations." These are not necessarily profound examples, but they do demonstrate meaningful changes in thinking. This exercise created a lot of discussion around how a project would change if we utilized some of these new words—it is difficult to deny that outcomes would shift. Step two of webwork completed: practise the power of relational thinking.

I discovered early on that if we were to have meaningful discussion about difficult and sometimes controversial topics, we would need a strong outer web that would hold us together as we began weaving the connections. A weaving process that could test the tensile strength of the thread at times. I try to strengthen the connection of those sitting in the circle to each other and to the issue at hand. It was a good friend of mine, Genevieve Singleton, the incredible teacher of all things nature-related and the person whom I thank for my connection to Cowichan Tribes, who best demonstrated this concept.

She had organized a gathering to discuss the management of the invasive knotweed on the Cowichan River, and began introductions of all who had gathered by having each of the people there not only say their name and affiliation but also name their childhood river or waterway and what they loved about it. It seems so simple, but was so incredibly transformative. It completely changed the room. We were there to work on a historically contentious issue and this single act brought everyone together. It made everyone relatable to each other. It connected each person with a memory that took them to a special place that they care about and put them into the ecosystem. Every land healing meeting or planning session I am part of now, I do this. Step three of webwork completed: bring the circle together and strengthen it.

Now that we have connected those in the circle, we can begin weaving what can be a multitude of webs. This is what webwork is about. Strengthening our recognition of the many connections each relation has and then figuring out what connections are required for the desired ecological balance. This leads us to the first question of webwork: Who are our relations in this place to which we wish to bring healing? Remember, Indigenous ecology requires us to honour the nature of our Indigenous languages even if we do not speak them. We therefore do not objectify our relations. All are equal. The trees, the soil, the insects, the birds, the plants, the nurse logs. We must acknowledge them as living and equal.

To show our respect for our relations, I have Healers in the circle acknowledge all the relations they can think of by naming them. Instead of objectifying them as nouns, they must be named as "Indigenized nouns." Similar to the examples provided by Robin Wall Kimmerer in *Braiding Sweetgrass*, our relations will be "bearing" instead of bears, "salmoning" instead of salmon, "rivering" instead of river, as examples. This practice is meaningful as it acknowledges them while bringing to the forefront of our consciousness their roles in ecosystem balance.

While we make these acknowledgements, we create a web with yarn between us. This is how it works: Each person who speaks holds a ball of yarn. As they name a relation, they then take hold of the yarn with one hand (point of the web) and toss the ball of yarn to another person in the circle, who names another relation. The circle keeps going so long as relations can be named. In time, a web forms. I use this tangible demonstration of relationality at each step of *webwork*, and encourage each web to be photographed. These material demonstrations of relationships can be powerful to share as a visible application of an Indigenous ecology. Step four of webwork well under way: the weaving has begun.

Now we begin the circles within the circle. We choose a relation—the humans, the soil, the salmon—and we create a web for them. This time the web is formed based on acknowledging their relationships with the place to be healed. A web of their relations. Let us use salmon in a riparian area and stream as an example. We may speak of their relations such as the invertebrates in the stream that they eat, the oxygen in the water that they need, the nutrients in the water from the vegetation along the stream bank, the shade the trees provide . . . This is meant to be both broad and specific. Its illumination of the density of our mutual dependence and our interrelatedness is almost always surprising to people. I will repeat this webwork for a number of our relations to continue to ensure that we remain in an Indigenous worldview, and that we are giving appropriate consideration to our relations as we work toward finding the desired ecological balance.

The acknowledgements and consideration that webwork accomplishes lead us to our most important question: *What is the desired balance for healing the land in this place?* This may seem as though it would be an obvious question to ask before embarking upon land healing efforts, but in the case of ecological planning that I have been part of, it is often forgotten. To be honest, I'm not sure I've ever been part of a project that asked that question. Upon review of numerous restoration plans from across the world to inform this research, I noted the same mystifying absence of this question. At first, it seemed to me that this really should be the first question that we ask as we begin any land healing journey. What I have learned is that the question of what the desired balance should be, or, generally put, what the desired solution to the challenge at hand should be, is the final question of webwork.

The webwork is the preparatory journey that acknowledges and considers all the relations and relationships, the necessary steps before making difficult decisions.

Our modern ecology has reached a place where "live and let live" for those that belong and a militaristic approach to those that do not has become the dominating force shaping environmental action. If modern ecological restoration is simply trying to put things back the way they are "supposed to be," then I suppose it makes sense that there is very little need for discussion of land healing goals. *This is so fundamentally wrong*, and it's the reason why projects fail. Precious resources are wasted on projects doomed to fail in the current context. Purposeful balance is not about everything having a right to survive. That may seem the easier and more righteous path, but we can see it is not the path to resolving our current ecological crises. Tough decisions and accountability to our relations are required for real change, and this is why traditional frameworks for ecological inquiry must be replaced by relationally focused webworks.

WHAT IS THE DESIRED BALANCE?

So often it seems that we jump instead to answer the question, What can we do to create the desired balance? Likely because that is a much easier question. Too often it is the only question asked because we assume what the goal of restoration should be and ultimately avoid having the tough conversations that require uncomfortable actions. In some cases, I don't even think people involved in land healing are aware that they are avoiding anything at all. When we understand an Indigenous ecology, it is evident that we must step up to our responsibilities as ecological leaders and do the preparatory work to be able to answer this very specific question, What is the desired balance? We should take heart that once we have done the difficult work of determining the goal, we can easily inform the action piece or target research at it. We are at the ready to tackle the logistics of the action pieces with our existing knowledges and experiences in land healing (formerly known as restoration ecology).

Prepared by the webwork we have completed thus far we now must sit in circle with this question as we gaze at the extensive and intricate weaving of relational considerations. It is within the web that we will find guidance, recognizing that there is no correct or right balance. As ecological leaders, we must do the work to position ourselves as worthy of answering this question of balance and be willing to be accountable for what happens as a result of our decisions.

I continue to make relationships tangible using the wool web-making exercise throughout these questions, even if tossing the wool is only a connection from one person's response to another to the question at hand. Following is the list of questions we used as we piloted the final steps of webwork. Questions changed based on the land or water healing project or the issue at hand. Again, these are meant to assist with guiding the process as we sit with all that we have woven together thus far.

What are the stories of this place?
What are our values of this place?
What is the current story of this place?
How are the relations of this place doing?
What connects us to this place?
What do we want the story of this place to be from this point onwards?

At this point, reflecting on the webwork completed, I ask the Healers to imagine the final weaving they created as an intricately woven three-dimensional tapestry of relationality. A representation of making whole this place we wish to heal. These final questions bringing the image to light, and the answer to "What is the balance of this place?" being revealed. One webwork participant likened these final questions to old-fashioned film development: "It was as though, through these processes, an image slowly began to emerge. Almost suddenly, there it was. Clear." I loved that analogy. It was a beautiful demonstration of relational learning. The final decision, what seemed as though it should be the most contentious step, was in fact the quickest and easiest. The weaving we create together tells the story already.

The story varies by project. Sometimes it is agreement over an otherwise controversial issue. Sometimes it is a purposeful new vision for a place. Sometimes it is acceptance of a change. I encourage participants to either draw or write a story of the new balance of this place to be healed. Let that be a final decolonizing act of the process, a subversion of the tendency in conventional land management processes to list priorities or develop some sort of hierarchical structure. Be mindful. Express the desired balance in a way that is reflective of the relational foundation of an Indigenous ecology. Use Indigenous artists to illustrate the desired balance that has emerged. Be brave enough to present your work in a new, relational way.

LEARNING THROUGH LESSONS

Just like Indigenous research methodology, webwork provides the freedom needed to weave connections together without a predetermined pattern. Our only goal is to create a web for the challenge at hand that is guided by our values so that we may consider our relations and relationships. The pattern of the web will emerge the way it needs to so it is reflective of the desired balance. The flexible strength of Indigenous research methodology is reflected by the flexible strength of webwork. Webs are never meant to be permanent. They can change or even be abandoned to create a new one. Much like our Indigenous stories, they too can adapt and change with the needs of our relations, ourselves included. Webwork empowers us to embrace change and adapt as we need to. This is the very essence of who we are as Indigenous people.

My teachings on webwork are meant to empower others to use a relational worldview to do good work. It would not be reflective of our worldview or of how our Elders teach us if I provided step-by-step instructions on how to use and apply it. That will differ depending on your subject area. I am only providing my own experiences as a "prepared beginner" who happens to work in invasion biology and ecological restoration. Our webwork, which I have called "values-based land healing," has provided an opportunity to gain new insights through a change in ecological philosophy. A return of ecology to its rightful, relational foundation. Webwork provides us with a guiding process to strengthen understanding and bring to light that which we may not have otherwise been open to see. The completion of webwork positions us to fill in knowledge gaps and reveal connections to bring about preferred solutions.

At last, we have permission to put ourselves into the ecosystem. We are free to find ways to honour our mutual dependence with our relations outside the confines of dichotomies and concepts of naturalness. Acknowledging the true history of our lands and waters, embracing our role as ecological balancers, and working from our relational worldview will give us greater assurance that we and our relations will have the resilience and adaptability needed as we face a changing climate.

There is much to consider as a leader, and ecologically, much is at stake in our world. The kind of decision-making that our planet deserves should be made by those worthy of that leadership, a leadership that is the opposite of dominance, and instead rooted in humility and great connectivity. It is a leadership that brings the people back to the land within our current context. One that understands the past enough to reclaim and revitalize the human relationship with land our Earth is crying out for.

9.

Living in Reciprocity with the
Land in a Modern World

BEFORE THE settlers found our shores, Indigenous ecology was simply the way people lived; with their arrival, that way of life was unravelled. Quickly at first, slowly and continuously ever since.

I had a dream one night. Our Earth Mother was made up of a tightly woven ball of twine. It connected us and held us together safely. It felt as though it was her perpetual hug and reassurance that she would always be there for us. Then I noticed her gentle but firm hold upon me was releasing. She was unravelling. The string being pulled with such a force that she was unable to stop it. I watched as she resisted as much as she could, but there was no stopping it. The unravelling became so much that she looked less and less like herself. I realized that she was getting frighteningly close to running out of twine. It was then that I awoke with a start, breathless and feeling the wetness of the tears on my cheeks and pillow.

I know I am not alone in experiencing the range of emotions that accompany the threatened state of our planet. Fear. Sadness. Helplessness. Anger. Yet, in spite of that turmoil, we are expected to just continue participating in a capitalistic society where our way of life has become one where we pursue jobs designed to pay this abstract thing we call money. We need that money so that we can go and buy what we need to eat (and other necessities). If we earn enough money, we might have some extra so we can then donate it to causes that are important to us. Causes like ecological restoration and conservation that can then afford to pay people to care for our lands and waters and other relations.

I'm sure you can anticipate where I'm heading. Let me start by saying that I am not here to debate capitalism. That is way outside my wheelhouse. I will assert that within the above two mentioned contexts, feeding ourselves and caring for our planet, it doesn't work. It. Doesn't. Work. Capitalism perpetuates the harms of colonialism. Protecting those who benefit from it while abandoning the needs of most everyone else, our planet, and all other relations upon it included. Ensuring all are fed is a value that is consistent amongst every Indigenous Nation I have had the honour of working alongside. I have heard it expressed many times, especially within the context of land healing. The two are rarely detached. If only everyone could exist within the alternative food systems of some of the Indigenous communities I see and participate in. Catching and processing fish, canning fruits and veggies, and following what my great auntie taught me about sharing what you have—a quarter for the Elders, a quarter for your parents, a quarter for others who may need it, and a quarter for your own family. I have driven cases of food around and, let me tell you, no one is forgotten. This is what could be possible if we could untangle ourselves from at least the parts of capitalism that leave people hungry. I acknowledge that this is not the case for every Indigenous community, but it shows that our ways have a lot to offer some of the most pressing issues of our times.

I hear a common criticism that we Indigenous folx have the tendency to romanticize the pre-colonized life of our ancestors and relatives. I don't think any of us have rose-coloured glasses on when it comes to the realities of what they endured and the challenges they faced, but I do think that this criticism is one that is constructed for two reasons: to defend systems of oppression that exist today, and to continue work toward the erasure of Indigenous Peoples. Here we are at a time of ecological crisis, and the systems that originate from those pre-colonized times, many of which have quietly persisted through genocide, clearly have something to offer when it comes to care for people and planet.

Within this dominant capitalistic society we endure today, mostly people feel detached from our lands and waters. Most of us can go about our daily lives and never consider or contribute to the health of our planet at all. This is not to make anyone feel badly; it's just what "progress" has gotten us to. Many folx are just trying to make ends meet and don't have the time or resources to factor in environmental health on a daily basis. Conversely, a conservation area or ecological restoration project probably isn't putting food on the table for most people either. Just as the people are detached from the land, care for the land is detached from the people.

A life of reciprocity with our land and waters is not the life most people can live today. It is not the reality of our world. However, there is much awareness today that the health of our planet is important. We are all collectively living in the consequences of human-caused climate change—we can no longer ignore it. Many people who don't do environmental work are comforted by the idea that people like me are out there doing the work that needs to be done—mending the planet, making a real difference. The truth is, we aren't making a real difference. There aren't enough of us, and there isn't enough money to pay us to do all the work. Even if we become more effective in our work as we apply an Indigenous ecology, *there are not enough of us out here doing the work*. Period.

Even those who consider themselves outdoorsy and/or environmentally aware find themselves in a detached relationship with our lands and waters. I spent a few afternoons at some of our provincial parks with my family, walking the trails and simply chatting with people walking by on the trail, being a friendly islander (embarrassing my kids). It wasn't formal research or anything like that, and I didn't write anything down. I was just honestly curious about where park visitors were coming from and if they engaged in environmental work.

It was overwhelmingly the case that people on the trails, whether they were on them frequently or infrequently, did not engage in any stewardship activities anywhere. I met one person who built trails for mountain bikers and justified that as ecological restoration. (Let's park that sentiment as it is important to this conversation.) If people weren't put off by some random person (me) striking up conversation, I asked more questions about their engagement with environmentalism. Some told me that they gave money to different groups or charities, or that they drove an electric car, or that they recycled or chose their food carefully to lessen their carbon footprint. All three days that I did this, I didn't come across a single ecological restoration volunteer or park steward—and by *steward*, I mean someone who engages in caring for lands and/or waters more than a couple of times per year. I did come across many people quick to make excuses and justifications for their lack of getting dirt under their fingernails.

Now, these conversations were not meant to provide sound empirical evidence. They did, however, point to my own experiences working in ecological restoration. The people remunerated for this work are few. They mostly work for nonprofit organizations as I used to (so aren't paid that much), and within those organizations, they then rely on volunteers as the workforce. Volunteers, too, were few and far between. In the years I have been engaged with local stewardship groups, I say with confidence that it is typically the same handful of people at every event. Local stewardship groups within communities of tens of thousands of people can only come up with the same seven individuals to clean garbage out of streams, pull invasive plants, and plant native plants—when we had the funding for them. Most of them have retired from being among the few paid environmental types, and are now getting on in age but feel compelled to keep going.

We are a society that has become only users of the environment, even if we see ourselves as "environmentally conscious."

Let me pull back the curtain on how many of our parks and "natural" spaces are maintained and run Wizard of Oz–style. There's likely a single person behind all of it. I have spent a great deal of time working with and volunteering within parks where I live and work. Would you believe it if I told you that there are fewer than three rangers for parks servicing more than a million people per year? Or that the person rescuing someone in a broken-down boat, managing dangerous wildlife, coordinating restoration projects, and enforcing park rules meant to keep visitors safe is often the same person cleaning the toilets? There are undoubtedly variations in terms of allocation of resources, but I'm willing to bet if you asked any park ranger anywhere if they had enough resources to steward the places they work, they would say no. Their work could be categorized as prioritizing park user safety, park user management, enforcing park rules, and maintenance. Stewardship is something reserved for when there might be time, or for when they can engage with an environmental nonprofit that is coming to do an ecological restoration project. They will tell you, though, about those seven people who come out for every event and help out. They are always grateful to their park champions. All seven of them.

Resources—human and otherwise—are limited. However, owing to the colonial vantage point of "set it and forget it" when it comes to the environment, people often don't realize that "natural" places require a lot of resources and work. Caring is not enough. Awareness is not enough. I have been part of successful environmental education campaigns for years, and many of them sparked public awareness and reports to government agencies about invasive species on government and private lands. When the public saw no or little management, then the calls started pouring in about nothing being done about their reports. Now, in many cases, we have a frustrated public who feel they have done their part to learn about the issue and report it to someone else who is supposed to, within this broken system of stewardship, deal with it. We drum up support for environmental causes, but there is insufficient action. Because the action is up to someone else. The few behind the curtain.

This is the problem of the few, the lack of resources, and the detachment between everyday humans and our lands and waters. We have created an environmental awareness that leads nowhere other than the occasional protest or a changed vote in a ballot box. As guilty as you feel about your inaction, I feel guilty about drumming up that awareness without having an action piece ready for you. I realize now that to alleviate my own and others' ecological guilt, a guilt associated with the knowledge that we can't do enough, we create a facade of a movement to make it feel as if we are doing something. It feels terrible to admit that to myself. In sitting with that, I have changed my tack. The question I ask of myself now, as one of these few who gets paid to do this environmental stuff, is "What am I doing to create better relationships with lands and waters?" Followed up by "How can I get more hands upon the lands and waters?" So, I ask you, as you sit with this, to ask yourself, "How can I get my hands and the hands of others upon the lands and waters?"

If we are to truly free ourselves from the colonial chains of modern Eden ecology, then we must *act*. There is no Indigenous ecology without personal reciprocity.

This is about creating opportunities for the ceremony of action. Working together to build into other systems the ceremony of land stewardship, asking what the community needs from the lands and waters, and building that into the stewardship. At a time when we are more aware than ever of mental and physical health issues, where our minds and bodies are calling out for help, it is not a coincidence that our planet is also in distress. Heal the people, heal the land. Heal the land, heal the people. This reciprocity is not for others to engage in on our behalf, and it is okay for us to shape the land to provide for us.

To reimagine a connection to the land, we must reclaim our role in the ecosystem in ways that fit our current realities. An adapted reclamation. These opportunities for engaging in the ceremony of healing land and people will look different than they did before colonization. The thing is, establishing this bond is not as difficult as it sounds. The past few years of extreme climate events and a global pandemic magnified both the "holes" in the fabric of our society as well as our incredible ability to pivot. Issues such as community food insecurity, supply chain disruption, lack of community connection, and compromised mental and physical well-being all came to the forefront. We collectively demonstrated an ability to pivot in the different approaches to the education of our children and young people, the diversification of our food systems (remember the bread making, and the canning jar and seed shortages?), and how we can connect with people in meaningful ways in outdoor spaces. Within our lifetimes, have we ever had such an opportunity to assert that "things can and should be done differently"?

Why are we trying to heal our planet? A question that may seem obvious . . . but is it? When we talk about reciprocity, are we remembering ourselves, the human relations? It dawned on me the other day that my work in agriculture has been distinct from my work on ecological restoration. It was a bit of a sobering confrontation as I've been actively working on bringing down the wall between the two. Their division is a direct reflection of the problem of colonial-era relationships with land. Agriculture equals food. Forests equal wood products, homes for critters, and recreation. These distinctions are plainly visible; you need only to fly over any land mass in an aircraft to take it in. The cleared squares surrounded by forested areas that often then run up into the mountains (at least where I am from).

Week after week, I found myself fighting off the plants of the forest seemingly invading our farm. It should not have been a surprise as we are surrounded by a coastal Douglas fir forest. It was a strange transition for me, however. I grew up around conventional farming area—flat, cleared land, very few coniferous trees. My move to Vancouver Island made me confront the question, What is a weed? I was not pulling the expected characters like dandelions and thistles; instead I found myself pulling mostly the native species I used in restoration projects when I lived in the city—trailing blackberry, thimbleberry, sword ferns, Douglas fir and maple seedlings, and salal. After dumping what felt like my hundredth wheelbarrow full of "weeded" forest species onto our burn pile, I walked slowly back to our food-growing area and thought about how my daughters and I should go and harvest some of the trailing blackberry in the forest later. I actually laughed out loud at myself. Here I had spent an entire afternoon pulling the very species I intended to harvest elsewhere later. Why? Because somehow I had been conditioned to respect this colonial line. Our Indigenous foods did not grow on the farm, and our farm foods did not grow in the forest. A truly bizarre realization. Since that day, I have begun allowing the plant relations of our forest to grow alongside our traditional agricultural crops. Trailing blackberry weaves its way along the edges of our thornless blackberries. I cultivate them both. Salal has appeared through our deer fences and I water it and we include its berries in our strawberry and grape jam. The abundance of deer has made it a challenge to reciprocate outside the fences, but we do have some herbs happily growing out in the open. Suddenly the dividing line between our foods—those of the forest and those from the farm—is a meandering mash-up of traditional and agrarian foods. I love it. I love it even more when friends visit and remark that they didn't know that you could eat a number of our plant relations from the forest.

My vision for Indigenized agriculture would be to fly over food-growing areas and see less distinction between these two landscapes. As a farmer myself, I know that there are some crops that require these large, cleared areas; but I also know that our own farm is struggling with the increased soil surface temperatures and water shortages that have come with a changing climate. I can see the benefit of increasing the vertical structure on our postage stamp–shaped farm surrounded by forest, and I feel some responsibility to increase our carbon storage. In talking to other farmers, I have been surprised at their support and interest in this vision. There is interest in increasing crop diversity to include culturally important plant species, and in being part of the #landback movement to grow foods and medicines alongside the Indigenous communities whose land they farm on.

It took moving to a rural community on Vancouver Island for me to see that what are often referred to as traditional food systems—food systems outside of agriculture or purchasing food in a store—play an essential role in the health of non-Indigenous people too. While I have always had friends who hunted, I heard about their hunts in the context of the good times they had. I categorized it more as a hobby, not so much as an important source of food for them. My cousins hunt and fish on our traditional territory, and I always put *that* in a category of exercising our sovereign rights and existing in a completely different food system than most of the rest of the people on Turtle Island.

I live in a place with the lowest median income in our province, and that traditional food system is a lifeline. Many of my settler friends rely on filling their freezers themselves with the animals they hunt and the fish they catch. This is how they can manage to feed their families; yet in every single food security discussion I have sat in over the years, there is never a mention of the value of this system. A system that also creates other opportunities to get what you need through the trading between families: canned goods for frozen meat, fish for garden veggies.

This traditional food system, not unlike the system existing in many Indigenous communities, is crucial to rural areas, but it is a practice that folks in urban centres typically have no connection to and may be critical of from a conservationist perspective. A phenomenon I find so incredibly telling of how far we have come from understanding the human role in the ecosystem. The division in our existences, urban to rural, so often rests upon this perceived separateness from the land. When the rules and environmental values seem to come from urban centres, those responsible for and participating in their assertion rarely anticipate the effect of their Eden-based, modern conservation values on those who live more closely to an Indigenous ecology. When the ecological high ground is weaponized against those feeding their families from our lands and waters, we only sow the seeds of unnecessary societal division.

My own move from an urban centre to a more rural island community was pivotal to seeing how we need to transform our relationship with land. In all my years talking within a settler context about food security, traditional food systems have never come up as a solution. The colonial concept that our food system is strictly agrarian is a haunting reminder of the perceived notion of settlers that our pre-contact lands were unproductive and "wild." This continues to permeate our perceptions and consideration of food security issues and how to improve them. Foods produced in "naturalized" areas could be a way to fortify not only ourselves but our relationship with the land too. By addressing food security outside of the agrarian setting, we can establish the mutual reliance needed to ensure mutual thriving. As a solution to both food insecurity and land care, these systems are especially relevant in communities most vulnerable to supply chain issues due to climate events. What if our land healing efforts were done from a food systems lens? What if we could find out what communities needed and conduct our land healing work according to the fulfillment of those needs? What if we factored in human need when choosing which species to grow? What if we designed projects so that they could get the care and stewardship that they require to flourish? It may be unreasonable for most people to work the land all day long in exchange for some food, but what if there were other needs we could meet through that stewardship work?

Over the past couple of years, I have brought students in ecology out onto the land, propagating traditionally important plants, weeding, planting, shaping the creation of adapted ecosystems, and called those activities lectures and labs. I have hosted collaborative work meetings unrelated to ecosystems while removing invasive species. In these experiences, we have stewarded land while doing the everyday, normal things that modern society tells us we have to do. Meanwhile, the land gave back more than just lessons, community, and mental health benefits. Students took home vegetables and fruits and herbs that they learned to process into medicines. Students learned food processing techniques and took these home with the instructions to give one jar away to a neighbour they didn't know and keep one for themselves, and this generated all kinds of discussion later about the people they would not have otherwise met. Many of whom came by and gave them something in return.

For years I participated in the failed stewardship model as one of the lone rangers being paid and overworked. Scraping together volunteers who were fatigued by the endless work with little in terms of tangible reward. I worked from place to place to place. Never for long. Never in a committed way. There wasn't time for such commitment. We had to get on to the next place. That's how the funding structure worked.

One day, I sat at the edge of a trail that cut through my research site, simply taking in the everyday routine of the place. I got to know the morning dog walkers pretty well as protocol meant I had to finish my work in the site by early afternoon. Eventually I could predict their order in a way that reminded me of the movie *The Truman Show*—red jacket black dog, yellow jacket grey dog, black jacket Jack Russell terrier. I began to learn their names and would greet each of them, and they eventually recognized me, too, and seemed to excitedly anticipate our encounters. I began to ask the dog walkers what they knew about the site, and like my park user pseudo-study, I asked them if they did anything to help this place that they seemed to walk through every single day. By now, these folks knew me and why I was there, and the common response was that they would help if they knew what they could do. I asked, If you were able to access food grown on this site because you'd helped out with the invasive plant management or watering or planting in the fall, would that increase the likelihood that you would contribute? "Of course it would!" was the almost unanimous response.

Now, would this come to fruition? I have no idea. But it made me think that our way of engaging with community and incentivizing people to help out would be transformed if we changed the nature of their relationship with these places they frequented just a little bit. This trail could be more than a throughway full of weeds and more of a community gathering and food hub. I can't help but wonder, if I had spent my time differently in those environmental nonprofit organizations—working as hard as I did not dragging heavy plant pots across wetlands, but instead putting that energy into reimagining humans' relationship with the lands where they lived—how much different our long-term project outcomes could have been.

The dog walkers became a symbol for me of the broken connection between people and land, and land and people. We can walk the same places every day and know little about how to help them. No one ever asks the dog walkers how their relationship to the land could be strengthened, or if they would make time to help out, or if they would like to see the land as something other than a path to walk their dog. Our environmental public awareness campaigns aren't empowering people to care for the land and they aren't empowering the land to take care of the people. If we free ourselves from the confines of Eden ecology, we can see ourselves as land stewards in the modern context. We cannot simply accept that there are only a handful of volunteers to steward those lands. It's on all of us—the youth, the dog walkers, the recreationists, the hunters, the fishers—to foster that reciprocal relationship.

My work with educators on land-based learning proves to me that stewardship specific to place can be accomplished with our kids. Not just planting trees, identifying plants, pulling invasive species, but planting food plants, caring for them, harvesting them to bring home, and preparing them to feed their peers at school. The stewards should include anyone recreating on the lands and waters. What if we reimagined licensing? What if there were stewardship hours required instead of fees? The stewards should be the dog walkers, having to pull a few weeds to put in a bin as they walk through. The stewards could also be those going for their morning coffee with friends, receiving a free coffee for working together on collecting seeds from plants. What if opportunities to bring community members together regularly to commune with one another involved getting dirt under their nails?

We need to create the societal infrastructure to build this relationship into our daily lives. The connection to specific places and the people who live among them is important and it is okay to shape these places to give back to us while they give back to the other relations that rely upon them. An infrastructure for stewardship tells all of us that relationship with lands and waters is part of your life, even if you are buying food in the grocery stores. It offers us a hybrid food system; confronts a conservation movement with the challenge of better understanding how human relationship enhances ecological functions; values the distinct needs of each community, whether it be urban or rural, and helps to meet them; and imagines solutions to ecological challenges that involve humans as part of the answer.

The loneliness and hopelessness I have felt as a steward on those rainy days, planting plants and getting soaking wet with a few other people, were not my own feelings. It was a cry from the land. The seven of us, planting only plants we had no relations to, were not enough. For a long time, I thought that the business of caring for land meant devoting myself to the pursuit of knowledges related only to that. One of plants and trees and soils. A pursuit of knowledge pertaining to everything in our ecosystems other than people. I was wrong.

If we are to apply an Indigenous ecology, then we need to move beyond awareness to reshape society to act in reciprocity with our land and waters. We know what the problems are; it's time for action and personal responsibility. Those responsible for land management need to be actively working on new systems that allow for citizens to engage in land healing as part of their daily lives. We have to make space for this engagement to be reflective of the specific values and needs of each place. If we are creating opportunity for land-based reciprocity that can help us to find and contribute to community, and increase access to local and more diverse foods, exercise, fresh air, and forest bathing, what other societal benefits await? This must be a transformation of human relationship with land, and not the disconnected patchwork efforts we have accepted as the best we can do. This must be a collective societal transformation that is reflected in a change in how people live their daily lives.

So now we return to the mountain biker I mentioned earlier in this chapter who claimed his trail making could be equated with ecological restoration. Is that ecological restoration? Where I live, mountain biking is life. Trails that are improperly made can cause serious issues, particularly as they change the hydrology of landscapes (how water runs and the consequences of erosion). So, many recreational bikers volunteer out on the land, acting in partnership with landowners, to build and maintain safe trails that minimize environmental impact. Through this, they are getting to know the territory well. While there is a strong connection to the land there, I wouldn't call this land healing; *but* I think it would be very easy for the landowner, in this case our regional government, to say that a condition of building the trails is that surrounding land healing efforts must take place.

The reciprocity of building something for recreational use is not sufficient. Perhaps empowering the lands around those trails to provide for our animal relations, or reducing fuel loads, or pulling some invasive plants, or planting tree species that provide food for all relations are some options. If we are already out on the land doing something, it is not hard to get the group to spend even an extra half-hour doing something else. Shaping lands for our own fun is important to strong relationship with land—it is just as important that we consider all our relations in that shaping while ensuring that we are acting with reciprocity.

For those of us who identify as environmental stewards, we are going to have to learn a new way of doing things too. Instead of fencing you all out of what we are working on, we have to figure out how to get your help to do the work, maintaining it and actively protecting it. None of this is easy, but it's incredibly powerful. How often have any of us asked, "What can I do?" when we watch yet another devastating wildfire, or flood, or slide, or see communities with food shortages. We might send money to help, but that is not helping to solve the problem. We must stop waiting for someone else to do the hard work for us. We must stop alleviating our environmental conscience only by recycling. We must demand that those who control the land start including us in her care. We must tell them what we want and what we are willing to do to make it happen. In an era that promotes "self-care," let us redefine that to include "land care."

Each night the same dream of our Earth Mother unravelling plagued me, to the point where I had become anxious about sleeping. Then one night, the dream began, but I saw there were a group of people, and they appeared to be working together. I could hear them laughing and talking to one another. Little ones playing at their feet. I couldn't quite see what they were doing, but there was a large wheel, and they were going back and forth to it. It appeared as though they were bringing things to it. Some coming from nearby, others from farther away. What they were holding appeared to be of different colours. I watched as the wheel turned, and as it did, I felt as though I was rotating along with the Earth. I realized I was being wrapped in a twine coming from that wheel that was covering the surface of our Earth Mother. It did not look the same as the twine I watched unravel, but it appeared strong and plentiful. The bright colours filled me with hope and joy again, and I felt snug and secure once more. Like a baby wrapped to its mother. I awoke gently to the dampness of my pillow from the tears rolling along my cheeks past my smile. I never had the unravelling dream again.

Part Four

Head Meets Heart in the West

WE NOW carry teachings that have brought clarity in our knowledge, empowered us to reclaim our ecological role, and given us the gift of the power to dream of ecological change. It is here in the western direction of the medicine wheel where it is time to reap what we have sown. To begin a new trajectory for caring for our lands and waters, a new trajectory for ourselves.

10.

Ye'yumnuts, My Teacher

*You are walking on sacred and hallowed ground to our people
and you come on here and bring in whatever it is. You gotta
remember that not even a foot and a half deep, someone's
soul is sleeping there. So don't forget that.*
Knowledge Keeper Harold Joe

YE'YUMNUTS IS the place where I found Indigenous ecology.
I am purposeful in my word choice when I use the term *found*
rather than the term *discovered*. There are two reasons for this.
First, the connotation of the word *discovered* rattles me to the core
of my Indigenous being. *Discovered* is a word that has been used
by settlers to erase the true history of Turtle Island, and I refuse
to use such a term to describe my contribution. Second, what I
have done, applying an Indigenous worldview to ecology, has
been done before. It is not new. It is how we lived before contact.
Other Indigenous knowledge holders are aware of this and have

done work in a similar vein. My contribution is in expanding its reclamation through my examination of what it means and how it changes our approaches to land healing and applied science in general, applying terminology to it, and providing guidance on how others can use it themselves.

Ye'yumnuts is a sacred ancestral site of the Cowichan People located in what is now referred to as Duncan on Vancouver Island in British Columbia. It is because of this place that I met Luschiim and other knowledge keepers important to the reclamation of an Indigenous ecology. Ye'yumnuts stretches alongside meandering Somenos Creek with gradually rising hills and a meadow that captures the sunlight perfectly. In recent history, it was simply another site of neglected land slated for rapidly expanding residential development in the area. It would have become another piece of the suburban neighbourhood that now surrounds it had it not been for the uncovering of archaeological evidence of the ancient village site as development began in 1992. Since then, extensive archaeological work has occurred in the area, revealing signs of human presence that spanned over 1,300 years, from 2,080 years ago until approximately 800 years ago.

Ye'yumnuts was the primary site of my research for my PhD, and I learned in the company of the Cowichan ancestors resting there, their presence made known to me in ways that would go beyond the comprehension of most. I cannot help but feel that they very much had a part in the many revelations along my research journey. For me, it could only be their guidance from the other side that steered me in the direction I ultimately took. A gift, it turned out, far greater than any results I would have received from the original intentions I set out with. It was here I learned to listen, to use my senses, to focus on relationships, and to realize the

importance of the true histories of the land to inform land healing. For me, it was all a tangible demonstration of relationality
spanning not only space, but time too.

My dad used to say to me, "There is always the right teacher
for the right moment." My hope is that Ye'yumnuts is the
teacher who helps you to bring together your webs of understanding of Indigenous ecology and our relational worldview.
That what Ye'yumnuts shows you intrigues you enough to consider how our relational worldview can change how you see and
approach your own work, your own relationship with the lands
you live on. This is the recipe, I believe, that will help to illuminate new paths of inquiry as we face increasingly complex problems in our world. The gift of reclaiming a way of seeing is to
truly make the stagnant new again. In this case, I hope that what
we have done here can help chart a course toward meaningful
and lasting ecological reconciliation.

While I had set out with the intention of studying impacts of
invasive species on traditionally important plant species and providing a decision-making framework for approaching ecological
restoration of sensitive Cowichan Tribes lands, it turned out that
Ye'yumnuts had much more to teach me.

YE'YUMNUTS AND THE COWICHAN PEOPLE: A BRIEF HISTORY[56]

> *Our ancestors touched the lands, rivers, and oceans*
> *in our territory lightly and with respect.*
> Luschiim

The Cowichan People have been upon their lands since time
immemorial with archaeological evidence dating back 4,500 years.

They are the Hul'qumi'num' People, part of the larger First Nations groups referred to as the Coast Salish People. Their territory follows the shores of the Salish Sea of mid-southern Vancouver Island and includes the lower Fraser River on the mainland of BC. More specifically, their territory includes the regions of Cowichan Lake, the Cowichan and Koksilah River drainages, the regions around Cowichan Bay, Maple Bay, and Shawnigan Lake, the southern Gulf Islands, and the south arm of the Fraser River. Before contact the Cowichan Nation was a large population with estimates of fifteen thousand people. It was a nation feared as they were the most powerful tribe of the south coast of BC.

The Cowichan People moved seasonally throughout their territory to harvest food and trade. Summer villages included Lulu Island at the mouth of the Fraser River (the location of Vancouver International Airport) and a large village, Tl'uqtinus, located in what is now referred to as the Steveston area of Richmond. This is where most of the salmon fishing and trading with other Nations (including my own) occurred. Winter villages were located in Cowichan Bay and the Cowichan Valley on Vancouver Island where Roosevelt elk, deer, bear, and a variety of plant foods such as speenhw (camas) were hunted, grown, harvested, and preserved. Many of these practices continue today and many more are being reclaimed. The spring called much of the Nation to various Gulf Islands where fishing included other species, such as herring and skate, and marine mammals, such as seals. Deer were hunted and camas harvested as well.

Cowichan Tribes was part of the Cowichan Nation before the arrival of Europeans. The colonial government broke up the Cowichan Nation with their creation of the reserve system and the Indian Act. Today, Cowichan Tribes refers to Cowichan

Nation communities who trace their ancestry back to the communities with winter villages on the Cowichan and Koksilah Rivers and Cowichan Bay. The history of the Cowichan People is rich and prosperous and a testament to the resilience of Indigenous Peoples in the face of indescribable atrocities.

Before we get into the lessons that Ye'yumnuts taught me, I must provide you with a summary of its incredible and complicated history. This history will not only help you understand the reverence of this place, but also provide a tangible example of the impacts of colonial rule, which run deep. So deep that they have both interrupted and prevented our ability to care for and heal the land our way.

Part of the broader Quamichan Village, Ye'yumnuts was connected to Tl'ulpalus (Cowichan Bay) via S'um'amuna' (Somenos Creek). The Cowichan People lived prosperous lives there, connected deeply to their lands and waters that provided for them. Abundant rivers nearby provided salmon, deer, and ducks on the creek; camas was cultivated, growing on the hills shaded by Garry oaks and in the estuary.

Archaeologists have identified three natural divisions in how the site was used, using radiocarbon dating to create a chronology of Ye'yumnuts.[57] Extensive shell deposits far from the ocean suggest that, in its first period, Ye'yumnuts was a large settlement where many Cowichan people resided. You can imagine that shellfish and fish would have been brought more than five kilometres inland to the village to feed the people. Archaeologists have found possessions of the many people who lived there made from imported materials, including tools and blades made from dentalia shells and chert (a hard, fine-grained rock), and a cutting tool or weapon made from nephrite, indicating that Ye'yumnuts was a hub of commerce. The Cowichan people who lived here travelled extensively and traded with other Nations near and far.

One of the most interesting features found at Ye'yumnuts was a very large oval concentration of fire-altered rock, which was likely a large cooking area for substantial amounts of food, such as the camas bulbs that were grown and harvested there. This feature had charcoal from hemlock, cedar, and crabapple trees in it, and radiocarbon dating of some of this charcoal dated it to approximately 2,800 years ago, suggesting it was used during the time of the Roman Empire. Another cooking pit used hot rocks for cooking. These finds are incredibly helpful to our web of relational understanding regarding the diets of our ancestors and which plants may have been present on site. This particular pit, found within what may have been a house dug partially into the hill (known by the archaeologists as a "cultural depression"), was 0.7 metres wide and 1 metre deep. Remains inside it included berry species such as thimbleberry and blackcap raspberry (species we continue to enjoy today), as well as red goosefoot and sedges. Other remains came from a wide variety of fish such as herring, salmon, skate, flounder, anchovy, perch, dogfish, sculpin, and greenling. The ancestors who lived in the village had a wide variety of foods from the surrounding areas in their diets.

In its second major time period, from approximately 1250 to 1850, Ye'yumnuts was used as a cemetery. Work completed on the site confirmed that more than thirty ancestors were found to be resting there. Because of this, protocols are in place to ensure that we work respectfully at Ye'yumnuts, which is common for cemeteries in Indigenous communities; these include not being there in the afternoon, brushing off when leaving the site, and not consuming plants growing over the burial areas.

Additional findings from this time period suggest how far we (Indigenous People) travelled from our home communities and how important trade and commerce was. Archaeologists uncovered an obsidian microblade, and when the chemical structure of this small volcanic glass blade was tested, it was found to be from Newberry Volcano in Central Oregon, almost six hundred kilometres away. I was fortunate enough to be able to hold some of these blades and tools in my own hands as archaeologists showed them to Elders, and it was honestly one of the most emotional experiences of my life. It was to be teleported to those times and feel and hear what the lives of our ancestors would have been like. It was to see the ties of relationality reaching across lifetimes, hearing the Elders talking about what their grandparents had told them about these tools, where they came from, how they were made, and how they were used. Remembrances coming back in real time.

As we reach Ye'yumnuts's third division in history, the closest to recent times, we must acknowledge that this sad and traumatic time period, the time of colonization, is just as vital to informing our land healing as the archaeological record. To honour this place is to speak truth. While the archaeological remains from these times were likely lost due to farming practices that eventually became the primary function of the area, we know much about these time periods as oral histories are fulsome and strong.

Cowichan lands remained free of settler control for much longer than southern Vancouver Island. In 1852, James Douglas came to Cowichan Bay by way of canoe, but it wasn't until 1853 that a formal attempt at European invasion was made. Three ships of more than 130 men sailed into Cowichan Bay to demand the surrender of a Cowichan man suspected of murder. He was eventually handed over in an attempt to placate the Europeans. This strategy was only successful for a short while before Cowichan territory was stolen, beginning in 1858 when nineteen settlers purchased 9,880 acres of land in the Cowichan Valley from the colonial government for £2,470. An 1859 land survey laid out reserves for the Cowichans while claiming that the best land now belonged to the government. It is important to point out that no agreement or treaty between the colonial government and Cowichan Tribes authorizing the sale of their lands was or has ever been made. Imagine if someone showed up to your house and just told you it was no longer yours, but you can have that patch of dried-up grass down the street instead, where there is no house or food. Imagine there was nothing you could do about it.

Despite the resistance of the Cowichan People, the government continued to survey land, and Cowichan reserve areas shrank as prime land was allocated to settlers. It was the equivalent of thieves sizing up what they were about to take. The resulting theft left Cowichan reserves at 2,075 acres and settler lands at 45,000 acres. The Hul'q'umi'num' people were robbed of their villages, spiritual sites, graveyards, hunting grounds, fishing areas, clam gardens, planting areas, and berry patches. On their way to areas they had accessed for thousands of years, they met fences. Again, please imagine that your family home, passed down through generations, was suddenly not yours. That as you go to enter your own garden, you find a large fence with a No Trespassing sign. Imagine. Please.

Ye'yumnuts was one such place. In 1876 it was sold to Herbert Worthington by the colonial government for $470.40, then in 1877 it was sold to William Kingston, whose family farmed the hundred-acre parcel for almost a century. Much of the Garry oak meadows served as pasture for livestock, and other portions were cleared to grow grain. The legacy of their farming is still found here in its soils, which have clearly been enriched by agricultural practices as well as by the continued invasion of the prickly English hawthorn trees they planted there.

In 1971, the land was sold to a development group who had planned to build a subdivision in the area. Driving to the entrance of Ye'yumnuts today, you wind your way through a typical sub-urban neighbourhood decorated with the beauty and shade of towering Garry oak trees, a startling reminder of this invasion upon sacred ground that crept down the hill toward Somenos Creek. It is important to remember that the boundaries that exist today are artificial. They do not delineate between what was an ancestral village and what is not; they delineate where the devel-opment was finally stopped after a lengthy battle to protect what was left. In 1992, as the final parcels were prepared for develop-ment, Cowichan ancestors had their resting places disturbed and were unearthed.

Development was temporarily halted, emergency archaeology was initiated, and early studies completed using soil conductivity surveys revealed the existence of the ancient cemetery. Shortly thereafter, excavations began as the developers, archaeologists, and Cowichan Tribes partnered on the study. Once the items I mentioned earlier were unearthed and a better understanding of the site's history was obtained, Cowichan Elders requested that the ancestors be allowed to rest, disturbed no longer.

Extensive negotiations resulted as the developer wanted to continue some of the building while Cowichan Tribes wanted development to cease. Developers wanted Cowichan Tribes to buy the area they wanted protected—a suggestion that baffles the mind as the land was stolen to begin with. Archaeological studies continued and more artifacts were found. Negotiations continued until 2011, when the developer gave a portion of the land to the province of BC to be protected and an additional piece close to the burial site was purchased by the regional government, the District of North Cowichan, marking the end of development of what remained of Ye'yumnuts. It's difficult to comprehend the angst of the community throughout such a lengthy process. Can you imagine the cemetery where your great-grandparents rest being slated for development? It seems impossible to fathom that such a situation could possibly occur, yet it continues to occur for Indigenous communities. It continues to be acceptable to settlers and colonial governments to disrupt the resting ancestors of Indigenous Peoples if their resting place is inconvenient to modern notions of land ownership.

While great strides have been made to remedy this injustice, we have a long way to go. I ask you, as our ally: please sit with this notion and feel it. Please use this opportunity to see how colonialism continues to erase us to this day. Process the deep relationship between Indigenous communities and their land at this point in our journey together. To enter Ye'yumnuts is to enter a sacred place. Just as sacred as any place of worship or any other important historic site. Ye'yumnuts is older than St. Peter's Basilica, older than the Colosseum. Why is it that our sacred places do not get equal respect? So much so that we have to fight tooth and nail to reach some sort of compromised version of respect. I have deep admiration and love for the people who worked so hard to protect Ye'yumnuts. They are a testament to the resilience of our People as well as the importance of our allies.

Ye'yumnuts provided the opportunity to experiment with my newly acquired "prepared beginner's mind" to see what the application of an Indigenous worldview to invasion biology and ecological restoration revealed. I was free to test out a research methodology that centred respect, reciprocity, and relationality, and began to realize the methodology's potential for addressing complicated issues in scientific research, and in the practical application of land healing. While not all of what I learned may speak to you directly, it certainly contributed to what I presented in the previous chapters. I hope the following lessons offer you the precious insights they provided me.

THE LESSON OF PERMISSION

The first and most challenging lesson Ye'yumnuts taught me was about permission. In relational fashion, permission is woven into every other lesson of our time together.

It is difficult to leave behind all that you have been taught and how you have always seen things. It is risky to step out and away from all that you and perhaps your colleagues are comfortable with. In the eastern direction of the medicine wheel, we journeyed through a spiritual letting go of familiar colonial paradigms.

Ye'yumnuts taught me that it was okay to leave behind what I thought I should think and what I had been taught by giving me a safe context to push the boundaries of the Indigenous worldview. I was free to practise using the lens I had denied myself the permission to use for so long. This gift of the lesson of permission is one I think every researcher could use. We find ourselves so confined by the rules of research, the norms of our subject areas, and the deference to the thoughts of others as opposed to trust of our own insights. Even if we are aware of these tendencies and want to change them, where can we safely do so without fear of reproach? Perhaps we all need a Ye'yumnuts in our lives.

As I walked around what was to be my research site for the first time on my own, I took in the landscape. A quick scan of my surroundings made me shake my head at the mess of weeds. "I could teach a weed science course standing still," I mumbled to myself. As I continued to wander, I made my way over to a group of Garry oak trees whose feet were smothered by the vines of the invasive species, English ivy. I shook my head in disapproval, thinking, This will have to go. I looked up in awe at the mighty oaks stretching their giant arms out above me. I imagined they were reaching up as a call for help as the invaders attempted to smother them below.

Lost in these thoughts, I was interrupted by the sound of a loud hiss. Confused, I stepped back. Nothing of our usual fauna would make such a sound. I must be mistaken. It was then that I saw movement in the ivy that could only be that of a large and very long snake slithering quickly toward me with ever-increasing speed. Overcome by fear and a feeling of dread I had never experienced before, I staggered backwards, turned, and ran from the area. When I reached the main trail I stopped, doubled over, trying to regain the feeling in my legs and catch my breath. What the heck was that? My analytical mind ran through the possibilities. Someone's escaped pet snake? My wild imagination? The jolt of the experience made me feel as though I needed to leave immediately. I was already well aware of the spiritual power of the site.

I decided to heed the message and returned to the entrance, where I sat on a concrete barrier to collect myself and my thoughts. All my attempts at rationalizing what I had experienced failed. I knew deep down what it was. In the same way that I had suppressed my own Indigenous worldview in my work, I attempted to suppress the

acknowledgement of the profound spiritual experience of the vision I just
had. It was not an escaped pet snake. It was Sisuital, the two-headed
serpent. While normally considered a water serpent with supernatural
powers, I knew some Kwakwa̱ka'wakw drawings depict it with hands
that helped it to climb trees. Sisuital, a spirit of revival and transformation,
was bringing me a message from the ancestors. A very serious message.
You see, to look Sisuital in the eyes means that you turn to stone. It
is why I had to get away so I would not see it if it showed itself by
emerging from the ivy. It was a message that came to interrupt my
reflexive thoughts regarding the landscape; a shock to the system meant
to stop that "invasive plant specialist" reflex . . . forever. From then
on, I would honour the land by seeing it from our relational worldview. I
would not be so quick to judge.

Upon this realization, still feeling terrified, I called an Elder to
relay what had just happened and to get advice about what I should do.
He said, "You have learned the lesson. You are safe. Now you must
go back in with the fresh eyes you have been given." I hung up. Took
a couple of shaky, deep breaths. And I walked back into Ye'yumnuts
transformed. The ancestors with me.

Just like that, I stopped working reflexively. I could set aside
the automatic categorization and characterization I had learned to
apply to the landscape and all the things within it from my education and work experience. I no longer considered it a "landscape."
It was a being made up of many relations, many of whom I had
never even noticed before. With the permission to see relationally
came the freedom to work and think differently. I no longer
opened my iPad GiS program and placed a grid over the site from
which to systematically work. I stopped bringing my field note-
book to Ye'yumnuts at all. I would simply wander and talk to

the insects, plants, trees, birds, and the occasional dog walker. Occasionally I would find a place to sit and be still. Sometimes I would close my eyes and just listen, taking the time to get to know each other. There was nothing else on the agenda other than that. The old me, a self-described Type A go-getter, would have been completely stressed out by this notion. I am typically all about an agenda, action items, and timelines. There must be a purpose, an objective, to everything I do, fuelled by a nagging urgency, with efficiency being the ultimate prize. No more.

There was a strange familiarity to this new approach as I embraced it. I realized upon reflection that I had done this once before, at a place that is very important to my Tsleil-Waututh Nation friends. It was a place that planted the seeds of doubt about my work as an invasive species specialist and offered a glimpse of land healing from our relational worldview—but at the time, I did not have the words or understanding to articulate it as such.

It is clear to me now that the relational worldview was how my Tsleil-Waututh Watchmen friends worked. They didn't need permission to work in this way; they lived it. They knew every square inch of their land and all our relations there, right down to where they would be and when. While I worked with them, assigned to my specific invasive plant management task, I remember at first feeling the pressure of time. Why were we spending so much time looking around, taking in things as though we were tourists and talking instead of working? I see now that the time I felt was wasted was in fact the time that we need to take. I felt conflicted by this pressing need to rush to get my job done and how much I absolutely loved lingering, really connecting with the land and waters. It was beautiful to come to the realization that this experience I had, so many years ago, had come full circle such that these important teachers of mine were indeed connected.

Just about every Elder I have spent time with has mentioned how we don't listen enough these days. We are too busy thinking about what we want to say ourselves, filling the air with our voice. These reminders about listening were not only about having conversations with Elders or knowledge holders; I realized that we need to give ourselves the permission to take the time to "listen" in our work. What do our relations have to say? I recognized that I largely didn't know because I spent most of my time assuming what they had to say based on my experience and knowledge. It is the curse of the "expert" that we stop listening and start talking, losing relationality with our work. It demonstrates how quickly we objectify these "places" we work and reflexively apply templated solutions.

Ye'yumnuts said, "Shhhhhhhhhhhhhhhhh. . . . . ."

The drive, in today's world, for productivity makes it difficult to believe that we can slow down. I needed the lesson of permission so that I could not only listen but release myself from the belief that taking such time was unproductive. What is the tangible deliverable for spending the day "listening" to a work or research site? I say this to highlight that there is indeed a systemic problem in society that will make adoption of this practice a difficult sell. My hope is that my story of Ye'yumnuts may illuminate why it is important to provide ourselves the required freedom to explore our surroundings such that we are really able to take them in. To ensure that we do not devalue the taking of time to consider and ponder. To work carefully. To step lightly.

Ye'yumnuts had much to teach me and would show me what I needed to see if I let it. I realized that if I clung to my original, specific research question, I would not be able to hear or see her message. I needed to open the door for possibility, to embrace Indigenous research methodologies wholeheartedly, and set out on a journey without a specific destination, instead taking various twists and turns to find lessons where I could from my Elders, knowledge keepers, the plants, the trees, the waters, the soil, the birds, and the insects. That this was what was needed to make sure my work was "good." Good work did not lie in a direct answer to a specific question; good work was to pursue a meaningful journey that would provide the community the teachings they sought.

The lesson of permission gave me a new-found freedom to see and work in a way I never had before. This opened me up to so many incredible experiences, which helped me to understand the relations on the land and where the opportunities were to bring healing.

THE LESSON OF MUTUAL RELIANCE

I went to Belcan Islands to look for some medicine that was said to grow there. No medicine. The old people said the islands were just full of it, this medicine. But it's full of Nootka rose. So, no more burning, Nootka rose took over. So wherever there's ground, meaning there's soil. Lots of rocky places, just rocky. Nootka's there, there's ground there. But no quxmin. So some of the vegetation control was done with a fire so you could grow what you wanted to grow. But no more.

Luschiim

I sat within the boundary between Ye'yumnuts and the Garry Oak Conservation Area. It is a wide trail, more like a road, that is the boundary between that which has been conserved and that which has largely been neglected. Neglected due to no fault of its own, Ye'yumnuts sat without human relationship for a long time while its future lay in waiting for development; that development was contested, and now the site is protected. Behind me, up the hill, Garry oaks towered in the conservation area. My old inclination would be to compare the two. Likely to assign positive attributes to the conservation area and negative ones to Ye'yumnuts. With the permission to see relationally and work differently, what I saw couldn't be further from that. In fact, what I was able to see now was that both places needed human relations. Both were suffering without us.

The Garry oak preserve was, by all accounts, a lovely south-facing warm slope with the eerily beautiful trees dotting the meadow. It is said that these were the very trees that Walt Disney chose as models for the trees that appeared in the original animated production of *Snow White*. While I don't necessarily agree with his characterization of them as frightening, they do have a magic about them, with their giant limbs appearing like massive arms reaching every which way. No two alike.

Resources and a lot of volunteer time go into conservation areas like the Garry oak preserve, which sits above this arbitrary line drawn by government that I was currently sitting upon. The line divides in pieces what was, at one time, entirely part of Ye'yumnuts. A line that now provides a comparison between land with more human relationship (much time and care had gone into the conservation area) and land that is largely left alone. This demarcation provided a unique opportunity to see why

Creator placed us in the role of balancers of the ecosystem. The conservation area with more Garry oaks, native grasses, and bulb species was a visual contrast with the area now referred to as Ye'yumnuts with few trees and a proliferation of weeds. A contrasting level of human relationship in the current era. Each side of the line provided a tangible lesson on what a difference this makes, but a closer look revealed a truth far greater than what was obvious from the aesthetic difference.

In the conservation area, the meadows that should otherwise surround the Garry oaks were being lost to the force of plants—both native plants and those considered invasive. Snowberry, *Symphoricarpos albus*, crept toward and in some cases surrounded the Garry oaks, creating tall and impenetrable thickets. Attempts had been made to rescue young oaks from being smothered completely by this "native" species by cutting the snowberry around them. Varying degrees of snowberry presence in certain areas remained as evidence of control trials of the past to deal with an issue that historically would have been handled by controlled burning. What was happening here was something I had seen so many times before, and it was predictive of what would happen to Ye'yumnuts if we allowed the same application of modern ecology to occur. A restoration without the foundation of relationality that placed humans as the balancers, based upon an aesthetic notion of the past, but neglecting to plan for the long-term human relationship needed for the desired result. A situation made worse by limiting the required traditional land stewardship practices due to fear (of fire), and a lack of resources for creatively adapting those practices to give the land what she called for. A restoration without the mutual reliance needed to ensure the success of all relations. Humans included.

Sitting and considering the site, I began the practice of envisioning myself watching what would have been happening there in the past when it was once a Cowichan village. The purpose of doing this was not to act as a guide to reconstruct the past, but to gain a clearer understanding of what we see today. I imagined the busy nature of the work involved in managing what I came to see as the Cowichan version of modern-day farming. Meadows burned when required to ensure the sweetness of the ground and to keep the meadows open from the intrusion of canopy closure for what were essentially "bulb farms." Camas and lily bulbs provided important sources of inulin (a starchy substance) for the community, carefully tended through harvesting practices that ensured that bulbs remained large and healthy, with some moved around to maintain the populations needed to feed the village. I connected this to the cyclical nature of the activities on my own farm over a growing season. Purposeful work over each season that ensured an abundant harvest. As with my own farm, the shaping and care of the land to provide food attracted relations who then also called it home.

It was perplexing to me that the Garry oak system seemed to be treated as though it was a natural phenomenon instead of the example of human ingenuity it really is. It made me wonder: As we approached the restoration of these areas, why wasn't the human relationship put at the centre of the plans, beyond the pulling of undesirable species and the planting of those that have been found to occur in Garry oak systems? If I left my farm to its own devices, it would be no surprise when I eventually found myself standing in a sea of weeds. Human relation with these places could not end simply when the pressing of the "reboot" button was done, or even down the road when the money ran out, as it seemed to have done here.

Like so many of my other professional experiences at restoration sites, this was not a failure of intent. This was a failure of execution—not in its initiation, but in its lack of continuation. This is what I mean when I say that I could see both the conservation area above and Ye'yumnuts below calling for human relationship.

Garry oak systems rely on reciprocity. Not just the human labour that goes into planting species that may have once resided there or pulling the Scotch broom that has invaded—they need the intimacy of human *relationship*. Mutual reliance is what made these systems thrive. Their existence provided sustenance. Our reliance on that sustenance meant that we nurtured these places. There is no mutual reliance in conservation models; they lack such reciprocity. There is maintenance of an aesthetic for the benefit of our other relations, but we often leave ourselves out. A maintenance that may last only as long as the funding. A maintenance that may not know all the land practices used to shape it long ago.

Obviously, we no longer rely on the land as directly to provide our sustenance and thus cannot return to that part of our history (though in some cases our communities are reclaiming our food security and food sovereignty). It struck me as I sat in ceremony, considering the nature of human relationship with Ye'yumnuts and its future, that the critically important issue of food security had never entered into any invasive species or ecological restoration project I had been involved in beyond impacts to agricultural areas.

Many of the challenges we face with long-term success of restoration projects seemed as though they could be resolved by ensuring that our relationship with our land and waters is sustained over time. The question I pondered as I looked over Ye'yumnuts in the misty morning light had gone from "How do we fix this?" to "What can we do to strengthen human relationships with this place?" While food security was one possible way to do that, it could not be the only opportunity to deepen our relationship with this place for mutual benefit. It is interesting that we expect the results of our mutual reliance with the land in the past as the results of today's restoration goals. To put things back to what was isn't our context now. For all that we try to do for our Earth Mother, without a reciprocal relationship, success will remain limited.

If there was a message that Ye'yumnuts was trying to give us all, I really believe it to be this:
"We need each other."

The whole system of attempting to do ecological restoration with government agencies dooms us to fail. The money will run out; the budgets for environmental projects will be the first to be cut; the volunteers will burn out. Deliverables for funding always have to be sexy—but long-term care isn't sexy. The work of relationships isn't sexy.

As I walked up the hill into the conservation area, I turned around to look at Ye'yumnuts below. I breathed in deeply and smiled. What I saw down there was an opportunity to work in a new-old way, focusing on relationships of mutual reliance. It would not be an attempt to return to a time that existed before or a context in which we no longer reside, but a focus on the potential of the relationships of now. What do we need? What are our values that determine that? What do our relations need? How can we deepen our connections?

Those involved in the Ye'yumnuts project approached it with relational intuition, which helped to strengthen the site's link to human community. Students from the University of Victoria did work at the site that forged cultural ties and ensured the seeds of mutual reliance were planted. This work was not separate from restoration plans—it was all part of land healing, and self-healing.

ELDER DIANE MODESTE:
Chocolate lily, tiger lily, were all part of our food. We didn't have modern potato and other fruits and vegetables. If you didn't have them put away, you wouldn't have food for the winter. You had to look after it and make sure it thrived. We were all part of it. Sometimes we would leave it alone for a while. Several years. To let it replenish for ourselves. We grew up with caring for what today is called "the environment." Caring for our land. Our stores. It was all part of our learning.

THE LESSON THAT HEALING THE LAND IS MORE THAN
ECOLOGICAL RESTORATION
The potential of Ye'yumnuts to demonstrate land healing done "our way" excited me. The notion that our values and our relational foundation could guide us made me feel as though we could finally resolve the challenges many such ecological restoration projects faced. Land healing was more than just fixing habitat for our other relations—it was about interconnectedness.

LUSCHIIM:

Everything is what sustains us. Everything is interconnected on this land. Even though we don't eat the grass, the deer eat certain grasses. Even though we don't eat that worm, they keep the ground aerated. So everything's got a purpose. That quote is from my mother. My mother said it perfectly. Everything is interconnected.

My time at Ye'yumnuts helped me to see that this interconnectedness was not just about connections between relations—it's also between concepts, categories, and understanding. All are required for healing of the land. Being balancers of the ecosystem is more than a balancing of the trees and weeds and animal relations; it is a balancing of connection to history and culture. It is to balance the mental and physical health of our People. Even the balance is interconnected. The interconnectedness of this collective healing will be what drives and sustains us.

My friend Harold Joe plays the very important role of archaeological cultural consultant for Cowichan Tribes. He also fulfills the role in the community as a self-described grave digger and death worker and is deeply connected to his ancestors through this work. His presence was especially meaningful at Ye'yumnuts because it's a burial site, and we endeavoured to follow the proper protocols and honour the ancestors.

As we talked about what the site was to become and which plants we might plant there, he spoke of what the ancestors resting at the site needed. This had never been a consideration for me when thinking about planning a restoration project. What did the ancestors need? Harold suggested that it would be important to plant things that the ancestors would recognize, and noted that food plants cannot be harvested over the burial site.

We would also need to be mindful of deep-rooted plants and trees that could disturb the archaeological remains. While it would have been easy to just take these as simple instructions, they really started to shape how this land healing effort would be different. Honouring the ancestors was fundamentally important, far more significant than a simple planting plan.

Anthropologist Brian Thom graciously welcomed me into the fold with the students taking the Anthropology course he taught as they partnered with Cowichan Elders, knowledge holders, and school district staff to develop what can only be described as incredible interpretive opportunities for students. Their skills and imagination conjured a vivid picture of what life in the village may have looked and felt like. It was clear that the work they were doing was just as much a part of land healing as was the creation of a planting plan. Without establishing connection to place, how could we possibly establish the connection needed to care for the land into the future?

It was this idea of cultural connection to the land that greatly intrigued me. For so long I had seen restoration plans fail over the long term, and I wondered if this interconnectedness was part of the solution. Social sciences. Applied sciences. These projects could have run in parallel at Ye'yumnuts, and ordinarily they might have, but it had become blatantly obvious to me that they needed each other.

The success of the planting plans for the site, created by architecture students from the University of British Columbia and by the provincial government, depended on this mutual reliance. The intention was largely to restore what should reside within a Garry oak meadow and to suppress weedy species—what you'd expect from a normal restoration plan, including lists of appropriate meadow habitat plants and weed suppression techniques. The plans were quite comprehensive, and I was impressed by the depth of knowledge. While there was no doubt in my mind that the experience of the native plant nursery would lead to an initially successful planting plan, I felt that to look at the failings of what was up the hill in the Garry oak Conservation Area was to see Ye'yumnuts's future. Without continued human support, successes initially gained would be lost.

To treat the site as only an ecological restoration opportunity was to miss a chance to strengthen community connection to culture, to history, and to traditional plants used for food and for social and ceremonial needs—all important goals for the Cowichan Tribes. Restoring what was there before would not ensure the connection to and perpetuation of important cultural knowledge or strengthen connection to place beyond the admiration of the aesthetic.

Being responsible for the plant management plan and replanting list myself, I could see there was an opportunity to do innovative ecological work. There were opportunities to choose appropriate locations to plant food, medicinal, and technological plants in concentrated areas, mimicking things like berry patches that would have been tended by a family to whom they belonged. Opportunities for plantings that would provide interpretive and hands-on educational opportunities about specific plants, and their uses. Opportunities for demonstrations on using specific plants including their harvest, maintenance, preparation, and preservation. I saw this as more of a connecting opportunity than a planting plan, and lands staff agreed. It was an exciting prospect—with the perpetuation of this important plant knowledge into the future, we may come to rely on our old "stores" again, at least partially. The gaps created by colonialism in the passing of our knowledge, and the resulting disconnection from culture, needed to be filled to ensure that the needs of all relations, human and land, would be met.

At this sacred site, it became so incredibly clear to me that healing community and healing the land go together. We are the land. If we heal ourselves, we heal the land. The land can provide that opportunity for us. This was a beautiful example of reciprocity. Never again will I approach an "ecological restoration" project without addressing community needs alongside planning actions toward land healing.

My daughters and I walked along the creek that winds its way through our neighbourhood in search of cottonwood buds. It was spring and it was time for this annual family activity to gather one of our medicines. I watched with pride and admiration as we broke apart and the girls began searching on their own for the fallen branches with the buds we would pick off. We had been doing things like this since they were very little. For them, this is simply their lives. Each season marked by another gathering opportunity, the observation of certain plants flowering and of where the bears and salmon are and what they are doing. Each season of gathering, I talk to the girls about reciprocity toward the plants and trees we receive gifts from. As a parent, you never really know how much they take in. Parents go on about all kinds of things that seem to fly over their heads. They are twelve now, almost thirteen.

Where does the time go? I wondered as I continued working on my own, watching them downstream. They ended up working together, one finding branches and bringing them to the other at the container to pick the buds into. I was farther up the creek, perched up high, and able to overhear their conversation without them realizing I was listening. They were talking about the medicine tree. The name they had given to this one immense cottonwood tree that every year dropped many, many branches. They were talking about the medicine she helped to make. Then I overheard one say to the other, "You've taken enough from over there. We need to leave some for the bees." My heart swelled. They remembered. The cottonwood buds are a first food for pollinators. It is what they use to make propolis.

They continued working and finally stood up and called for me. I came down and we realized we had harvested enough. Hands on hips, one of my girls said to me, "Okay, so what should we do for the medicine tree this year?" Again, my heart swelled. Reciprocity was automatic for them. The medicine tree had given her dropped buds to our family to make healing salves and now it was our turn to give to her. I said, "What do you think we should do this year?" Last year we had pulled the Scotch broom that had begun overcoming the area. This year we noticed a few daphne laurel appearing, as well as what seemed like a lot of garbage that had flowed downstream onto the banks. The girls decided we would go back to the house, get the appropriate protective gear (daphne laurel is toxic) and garbage bags, and come back to pull the daphne and collect the garbage. When we finished, we said goodbye and thanks to the medicine tree. The girls said together, "See you next year!"

I share this story because what I have learned from my children, as well as from the children I have had the opportunity to share plant knowledge and traditional medicine making with through my kids' schools and Girl Guides of Canada, is that both they and the land have much to gain by finding ways of deepening their connection. This is not just by having them spend time on the land and making them learn the names of trees and plants (which they will often forget). This is about providing opportunities to strengthen their ties through things like teaching plant uses. Finding ways for them to see and experience how these plants and trees can provide for them and be integrated into their everyday lives. If we do this, children will maintain that connection and return the favour to the land. One of my favourite Guides, a super-keen and spunky character, said to me, when talking about what reciprocity was, "Well, it's only good manners! Duh!"

On another occasion I took the Guides out for a return trip to a place we had visited before, where we had talked about plant medicines and technology and I had shared some traditional stories about the standing people (the trees). We had made some salves the following week with what we collected. On our return trip, I had the girls do a scavenger hunt to find the plants and trees based on their uses and stories that I taught them on our first trip. I asked them to write the actual names of the plants and trees if they remembered them as well. What was fascinating is that they completely remembered the plants and trees based on the uses and stories, while recalling around 25 percent of the actual names. Knowing our plant relations through their relationships with us and our other relations placed them directly into a relational worldview. They were no longer simply part of the green background of being in "nature"—they were our helpers, and the helpers of other animals the kids liked. When I took them back a third time to remove some Scotch broom (an activity that had created much bellyaching previously), there wasn't a single complaint. They were going to help the forest that helped heal their skin. "Seemed like a fair deal," one of the girls said to me when I asked why they weren't complaining this time.

The children show us that by healing other parts of our lives, we can heal the land. We can create meaningful relationships with the land by simply getting to know it in a more personal way that compels action. These may no longer be our stores, but they can provide for us in other ways that fit into our modern world if we let them, and they may just provide the answers we need for improving community well-being. Our approaches to land healing must go beyond plant lists and tactics to remove weeds. In creating these relationships, a mutual reliance, we create long-term opportunity for the land to be cared for and the opportunity for us to be balancers once more.

THE LESSON OF RISING UP FOR OUR INDIGENOUS ECOLOGY

Upon expressing my frustration about failed ecological restoration projects and government hurdles to taking appropriate action to manage our lands our way, I asked Luschiim, "What can we do?"

LUSCHIIM:

What can we do? What are we allowed to do? It seems like every time we turn around there's rules and regulations and laws that prevent us from doing things. Yeah. And that's where we are. Yeah. So what is our role? Can we bull our way through and make our voice be heard? That's pretty well where we've gotta go.

This is where it gets complicated. Indigenous communities find themselves in a jurisdictional tangle over lands that are acknowledged as theirs and yet they have little control over them. I have sat in many multistakeholder meetings about issues of ecological restoration over the course of my career, mainly as an independent expert to provide guidance as the stakeholders work together to figure out what they may want to do. It was an entirely new experience for me as I sat in such a meeting about Ye'yumnuts, as part of the "stake" that Cowichan Tribes represented. I was invited to address the invasive species issues and determine the appropriate plants to plant based on my experience and the research I was doing. At least, that is what we thought my role was.

As I presented to the colonial government agency alongside my co-researcher partners, Cowichan Tribes, I felt dismissed. I felt unheard. I finally understood the throwing of hands up in the air that comes with the feeling of powerlessness. All things I had only ever observed in this type of context, but not personally experienced before. I was no longer protected by the shield of "expertise." In this case, I was just another Indigenous stake at the table to be acknowledged but not heard. It was a transformative experience, and one that hurt my heart. The very People of the land, who know the land, the People who have the power of a relational worldview, reduced to a box-ticking exercise.

I realized that every participant in that meeting was caught in the context of the legacy of colonialism and I'm not sure that the non-Indigenous folx recognized that their way of working perpetuates it. But it does. Ye'yumnuts is currently under the jurisdiction of the provincial government in spite of it being Cowichan Tribes' ancient village, and while there is an attempt to allow Cowichan Tribes to provide guidance as to what they would like to have happen with the site, this opportunity still exists within the hierarchy of colonial governance.

I sat in the meeting and tried to focus less on the back-and-forth between parties and more on the feelings the conversation was creating in me.

Frustration *is the best descriptor. I could hear our ideas come forward only to then be shown what they (the government) had already decided they wanted to do with the land with their contractor. It felt like more of a presentation of what we were to accept as opposed to actually working together in a collaborative effort toward creating a plan based on what our (Cowichan Tribes') goals for the site were. It felt disorienting as we didn't even know that a contractor had been hired. I tried to understand what had happened to get us to this point. It seemed to me that we, and those involved long before me, had made clear what we wanted for the site. I bit my tongue for as long as I could.*

Then I could hear Luschiim's voice in my head. "Can we bull our way through and make our voice be heard? That's pretty well where we've gotta go."

I tried to resist being the bull, but she broke free and charged right in. I cut off the conversation, which was heading into logistics of a plan that wasn't going to achieve our desired result.

I asserted our concerns regarding the plans, which had the potential to further introduce weedy species to the site, and added that their plan was not what was desired. Perhaps it was my own ego, used to being yielded to when sitting in these situations in the "expert" seat, but I felt completely taken aback by the instant and assertive dismissal of my comments. I don't think I have ever felt so minimized professionally. It was hard to take. As I looked around, my Cowichan friends did not seem surprised or shocked. I got it now. I understood.

I let myself feel sad for only a moment. Be the bull, I thought to myself. Be the bull, as Luschiim said.

After much back-and-forth, an agreement was struck that I could work with the contractor hired to complete the native planting plan. The contractor was clearly caught in the middle and unaware of the entire context. Meanwhile, the ministry's preliminary work to protect the archaeology would begin. Drawings were made of what this should look like. More back-and-forth that felt unclear. Then the meeting was over.

Time passed and I had heard that the early work had been completed by the ministry. I decided to visit Ye'yumnuts to check it out. What they had done was nothing like what we had drawn at all. It wasn't what we wanted. I felt confused and disappointed and frustrated, but, sadly, not surprised. We would just have to find a way to make it work.

This experience was a humbling demonstration of what Indigenous communities face in these types of land management consultations. Some will say, We've come a long way as now we are included in the conversations and "consulted." That may be true. Sometimes we luck out and get listened to. I have seen demonstrations of government agencies and staff that really do make it work the best they can. In fact, I have heard many of them complain that the entire system is set up to fail Indigenous communities. In this case, it certainly felt that way. Here we are, a site of such importance to the community, and the community doesn't have full control of it. This colonial process is most certainly not reconciliation.

At this point, I had already compiled lists of plants to serve the multiple purposes of relationship building that was to form the plan. Plants for ceremony, technology, food, and medicines. The contractor made space for my ideas as we collectively found ourselves caught in the middle of the strangeness of the situation. They are exemplary Indigenous allies trying to do the right thing. The planting plan that we wrote for Ye'yumnuts together resulted in probably the most decolonized version of such a plan I have yet to see. We incorporated Hul'q'umi'num' language and used some of the terminology I had developed that reflected Indigenous ecology. We included the cultural learning opportunities to deepen connection with the land. I was still mid-journey, so the document did not receive the full benefit of all that I have learned up to the point where I am writing now. I realize that the purpose of the entire exercise was to inform what I share with you now—an example of applying an Indigenous ecology that reflected the values and goals of the community and made use of the incredible expertise of all involved.

Having a reclaimed and revitalized way to see and approach land healing is one thing; the reality of the context of implementing it is quite another. Existing colonial governance structures, notions of land ownership, funding models, and modern ecology are examples of what can feel like a multitude of hurdles Indigenous Peoples must overcome as we move toward ecological reconciliation. Ye'yumnuts made me remember that resilience is who we are—our existence is resistance, as the common saying in my world goes. With Luschiim's words in the back of my mind, I embraced a new-found confidence in asserting our way of healing the land. This was not about disregarding other knowledges. This was about moving land healing onto our relational foundation so that those other knowledges can be applied and assured a more successful future. This was less a battle of wills and more a battle for the opportunity to be teachers ourselves.

Ye'yumnuts introduced me to so many allies excited by the possibility of doing things "our way." Upon our disrupting these regular "ways of doing," there was a captive and receptive audience. Many of whom expressed the same frustrations that I had with poor long-term outcomes. They too wanted a new way to approach land healing, and I came to realize that we cannot rise up on our own as the journey is difficult and long. We need the help of our allies, but without the necessary knowledge, they cannot help us. We must disrupt these processes in a way that creates the space we need to bring an Indigenous ecology to light. We can rise up as teachers to help folx work with us relationally, sharing values and frustrations. We may not win everyone over—change is hard—but we need to share this gift of our relational worldview so that we may successfully bring healing to the land.

THE ANSWER

In the beginning, I felt as though my research journey was failing as I had not received a clear or definitive answer to my original PhD research question of what the impacts of invasive species are on important food and medicinal plant species. For all my discussions with knowledge holders, any time I directly asked the question "What do you think about invasive species?" I received stories about an instance when one species provided something important, and then another when that same species made a medicine disappear entirely from a place where it had long thrived. Ye'yumnuts too, like any other good teacher, refused to make it easy or provide a clear answer for me. I would have to take what was shown to me and figure it out.

Sometimes it felt as though I was being given a riddle. As if it was some sort of test I was supposed to pass before I would be given yet another. I recall one of Luschiim's first meetings with me where he seemed to get frustrated with me. He made it clear that his job was not to give me any answers at all; his job was to share what he knew. I had to do the work to decide what came next. At first this responsibility felt heavy, like there was some great answer that I might possibly get wrong. After the lesson of permission, I let go of the heaviness. I was free. I trusted my teachers. I let the learning unfold in the process. That's why my research question changed to "How does applying an Indigenous worldview influence invasion biology and ecology?" Slowly but surely, by sitting, watching, and listening, the lessons became known. The connections were woven together. Just like the artifacts that emerged from the earth of Ye'yumnuts, so too did an Indigenous ecology.

11.

Storytelling to Connect Us All

CARRYING ALL the lessons that Ye'yumnuts taught me, I thought that the final piece, figuring out how to bring healing to the land, would be the simple part. I was through the hardest part—the unravelling of my Western education—and was reclaiming an Indigenous ecology. I would neatly weave it all together and tie the ends into a tidy bow. How wrong I was.

I was drifting in a sea of data, and not the familiar data of Western science. It's funny that analyzing that kind of data used to seem hard—now it seemed almost ridiculously simple. I found myself with that same data along with years of relational observations just sitting on the land, the knowledge of Elders and plant knowledge keepers, stories of all kinds, and the real histories of the Cowichan Peoples and their lands. How were pieces so dissimilar meant to come together? My research came to a grinding halt.

I took my worries back to Ye'yumnuts and sat alone atop the hill overlooking the site, hoping to get some sort of sign that would help me to figure out how it would all come together.

Nothing. I cried. And not like an elegant, gentle weeping. It was loud and cathartic and carried in the breeze over the land below. I felt crushed by the weight of the responsibility that came with these knowledges, and I felt ashamed. I had no idea what to do with it all.

I had spent weeks attempting to analyze all of it as I would data collected within the Western scientific method, trying to fit the stories and my observations together like pieces of a puzzle. Hadn't I even criticized bringing Western and Indigenous knowledges together in this way? I learned first-hand that it didn't work. I felt like a child forcing unmatching pieces together with my fist.

Because I was.

I sat in the depth of my own frustrations trying to find a way out. What was I so desperately trying to make out of those pieces that I would force them together like that? To treat these precious gifts I had been given with such rash disrespect? I realized I was so desperate to make something, *anything*, out of it all, to rush to finish this journey on a timeline of my choosing, that I was willing to make these lessons into the very thing I was trying not to create. A construct of the dominant worldview. In my rush to serve my own deadline, I had lapsed into Eden-based ecological restoration because that was easier. But it couldn't be done. The pieces weren't made for that.

The missing part of the grand puzzle of healing our planet was not about individual pieces, but the lens itself. A lens that could create the images reflective of an Indigenous ecology to guide the healing that our planet and all relations upon it so desperately need. Each image made specific to each place, according to the needs and values of communities. Images not solely of lands and waters and non-human relations, but inclusive of people too. I had thought that these images were to be made up of a blending of knowledges—Western scientific, Indigenous, and really any other knowledges of value. There had been so much attention recently on "braiding" and "weaving" Indigenous and Western knowledges that I was stuck within the confines of these analogies. How does one blend together things that are so incredibly different?

Consumed by this quandary, one night I had a dream.

I was holding a painter's palette, and I looked down at the colours in each well. They were the most beautiful colours I had ever seen. I am not sure what it was that I was supposed to paint, but I found myself attempting to blend the colours. I dipped my brush in one and pulled the colour toward another. Then I dipped the brush in another colour and pulled it to meet the first one. I swirled the brush, and I watched the brilliancy of each colour disappear further with each rotation. I tried to pull another into the mix in hopes of bringing back some of the brilliancy and perhaps create another colour I had not seen before, but instead that resulted in a mess of what looked . . . brown. The vibrancy of the colours was lost.

For some reason I felt this pressure that I had to blend colours to begin my painting. As though someone was demanding that I do it before I could begin. I don't know where this sense was coming from, but I suddenly shouted at it, "I am only painting with the brilliant colours!"

I woke up. I think I may have shouted in my sleep as I awoke feeling as though I had heard myself yell.

I understood.

These knowledges, they were not meant to be blended. They were not even meant to be braided and thus partially hidden.

They were meant to be individually and wholly seen and felt in the heart and mind. Each one was beautiful and had something important to contribute. No knowledge should have its integrity eroded by another. In this moment of understanding, I felt a greater mission. A greater responsibility. This wasn't just about figuring out how to bring these knowledges together; it was about ensuring their protection while doing so.

This research journey wasn't meant to be a puzzle, or a stewing pot, or weaving, or braiding—it was a mosaic. The images created by a relational, Indigenous worldview, the images meant to help us to shape our lands once more, were an assembly of knowledges, like what I held from my experiences at Ye'yumnuts. The Western scientific measurements, the traditional ecological knowledges, the local knowledges, the sitting on land—they were to be gathered and brought together through a web of possibility with a vision for the future in mind.

At the time of this realization, I had taken up beading. One day, as I sat with my beads in front of me and an idea in mind, I was trying to figure out how to bring them together. It dawned on me that this was a reflection of the process we had to figure out to heal our planet. The individual beads of each knowledge system needed to come together to form the picture of land healing we desired. Each bead contributing the very best of each knowledge type. Each visible on its own but brought together with the others to create something beautiful. We each contribute our beads as our allies contribute theirs. Science is better alongside each other.

One step forward, two steps back. I now had clarity about the nature of the image and the parts to create it; the problem was

I still had no idea how to generate the picture. Even if we knew what image we were hoping to create, who was the artist supposed to be that would bring it all together? Feeling desperate once more, I decided to shake things up and bring my children along with me one morning to Ye'yumnuts.

The freshness of the air hit us all at once as we got out of the minivan. We took a collective deep inhale, and exhaled in a way that I could tell connected us all with the earth beneath our feet. The dew was plentiful upon the tall grasses and the early morning sun illuminated the countless spiderwebs that decorated the Himalayan blackberry bushes lining the path below. We could hear the soft murmur of ducks on Somenos Creek along with the occasional splash of someone landing in the water. I had not brought the kids here before, though they had heard plenty about this place that I was disappearing to frequently for research. As we walked in, we brushed off and I applied ochre to their faces and hands to ensure our spiritual protection, especially my kids', in this ancestral resting place. I could tell this caused them trepidation about being there, so as I led them further into the site, I began telling them the history of Ye'yumnuts in a story-like fashion. Weaving in narrative about the kids their age who would have lived in the ancient village that once stood where they were right then, what daily life may have been like. Their houses, the games they would play with their friends, the foods they would have helped to harvest and prepare. The excitement of first hearing and then seeing a canoe coming up the stream bringing fresh clams. The anticipation that perhaps it was their father returning. They were clearly enchanted by this. Suddenly what appeared as a place full of weeds, an empty field mostly, had come to life for them. They began gathering up some sticks and playing as though they were acting out the lives of those who had been upon these lands a couple of thousand years before them. It was as though I could feel the lifting of the spirits of the ancestors there to hear the happy sounds of children across the village site. I reminded my children that we cannot be shrill or shout and that we did need to walk respectfully as this was now a resting place.

At this point, the story took the turn toward the colonial history. For my children, I remained in storytelling mode. Helping them to understand from their vantage point what happened to this ancestral site since the arrival of the settlers. I told them about how the Garry oak meadows, like the one at Ye'yumnuts, were the bulb "farms" for growing camas and other starch sources for the Cowichan Peoples. I told them how these farms were stolen and became prime grazing lands for the livestock of settler farmers. This particular area was home to cows for almost one hundred years. I told them about how Ye'yumnuts was almost swallowed up as a neighbourhood by the houses that currently surrounded it. How the Garry oaks in between the houses in those neighbourhoods tell the true story of the land and how big the village really was. I told the story of how the ancestors were disturbed and then returned to the land. I told them that now there were many people, myself included, working toward healing Ye'yumnuts. I was surprised by their interest and their very strong feelings about what I was telling them. The injustices were not lost on them at all. They expressed their own anger and disappointment at how anyone could treat other humans in these ways, in the past or now, and it fuelled an immediate desire from them to make things right.

I wondered aloud to the kids what Ye'yumnuts could be next and shared with them my frustration in figuring that out. I told them about how Cowichan Tribes' hopes and dreams were for the site to become a place where the ancestors can rest, but also a place of cultural learning. One that the children who attended the schools just on the other side of

Somenos Creek could visit and benefit from, for example. To be a place where food could be grown for community. We had been walking around Ye'yumnuts and ended up in what is referred to by colonial boundary makers as the "conservation area" up above. We found a place to sit where we could overlook Ye'yumnuts and the kids immediately took over the role of storyteller. It was as if they had caught on to the spirit of storytelling, continuing from where I left off, onwards with their own versions of what might well lie below us one day. Who would come there and what they would learn. I cannot separate and attribute each individual idea to each of my children as they collectively exclaimed all at once and collaboratively told their enthusiastic stories, all while pointing to different areas of Ye'yumnuts:

> *"Over there, a place where kids can sit and hear the stories of the Elders and learn songs and drum. And over there, berries to pick. And over there, a place to learn how to make our fruit roll-ups with the berries. Over there, a patch of camas that a class is responsible for. And there, a pit to cook the camas. They can plant carrots on that spot. Maybe some other crops too. Oooo, what about a place to do art?! It is so beautiful here, people will be inspired here."*

This went on in greater and greater detail for a passage of time I didn't dare check with my watch. It felt too special and sacred. Their excitement to create a story for Ye'yumnuts was infectious. They could see what I hoped to see but brought it to life in a way I hadn't been able to. It made me laugh. Peter Cole, the Indigenous scholar I mentioned earlier in the book who had provided me critical advice on Indigenous research methodology when I began my research journey, wasn't kidding when he said to find lessons from my children. Ye'yumnuts just used the kids to show me the way. Storytelling isn't just for teaching about something, it is for figuring things out too. Relational data analysis *is* storytelling, and it creates the mosaic image, in this case through the reclaimed lens of an Indigenous ecology.

I have used storytelling to reach students, the general public, colleagues, and politicians on topics such as weed science, invasive species management, and environmental policy. It is something that I know has made me an effective and compelling teacher. What my children taught me in this experience with Ye'yumnuts was that despite storytelling being my go-to teaching pedagogy, it was not something that I used within my work. I used storytelling to teach *about* my work but not as a tool to use myself *as* I worked. I did not see that my work as a restoration ecologist was really storytelling of the past, present, and *future*.

In *Braiding Sweetgrass*, Robin Wall Kimmerer raised the point that no one working from a Western scientific perspective asked the plants when approaching them, "What can you tell us?" as the fixation was on how they worked.[58] I propose that the next question—not just for the individual relations within a place, but for the place in its entirety, like Ye'yumnuts—should be, What is your story? What was the story of the camas that remained there? The Garry oaks? The creek? To ask "What is your story?" is to honour the past by acknowledging its truth and learning from it. To ask "What is your story?" is to honour the now by acknowledging the relations as they currently are and the web of relationships they currently have. We then must ask, What will your story be in the future? A question that honours the future of each of our relations here now while immediately highlighting the immense responsibility placed upon us humans, as shapers of the Ecosystem.

To ask Ye'yumnuts "What will your story be in the future?" would require us to author the story from this point onwards, to provide the balance required for that story to come into existence, and to see that the story is fulfilled. Perhaps this is the reason why Eden-based, ecological restoration is easier. If it fails, such responsibility and accountability are not woven into those projects. No one must wear the blame for the failure. The only accountability may be to the funders, but it remains easier to explain away the failures as the acts of a colonial notion of "nature."

I realized that the stories and knowledges shared with me and the observations I made were not meant to tell us how we move forward, nor were they meant to be instructive. They were imparted as ceremonies meant to connect us with the land, with essential learnings, with each other, and with our values. This was the work required to help inform the placement of those tiles or beads of the mosaic which each successive generation would ultimately be accountable for, because these images of land healing, they are meant to be like Indigenous storytelling. Ever changing, reorganizing, moving in new and unexpected directions, all to exist in the current context and to build resilience for the future.

I returned to Ye'yumnuts the following day without the kids. I said my prayers and thanked the ancestors for this lesson on the power of storytelling. Storytelling for the future, captured in an image meant to be an act of cultural witnessing, based in a language of animacy. Not meant to be admired from afar, devoid of human relations, as the modern conservation or environmental movements may have us believe, but instead depicting the multitude of relationships within a place and the responsibilities that come with those relationships. Every image is unique and compels action. The healing radiating from such images is not exclusive to our lands and waters and non-human relations—it is multidimensional, applicable to people and communities too. Healing ourselves is not separate from healing the lands and waters. Healing the lands and waters is not separate from healing ourselves. This is the medicine wheel for the planet.

I had a routine I followed with which I would move about Ye'yumnuts, one I had begun to hurry through. Now, I stopped at each point, sitting down for storytelling. I sat at the top of the hill, running my fingers through the soil, and said, What's your story? The soil told me about how it had changed over time. How care of the soil had changed from the time of the camas fields to the time when dairy cows dotted the landscape to now. The soils were anthropogenic, but in a way that suddenly felt far deeper than in any other context I had used that term before. These soils had been cared for and worked long before the agrarian intrusion upon this landscape. What did this mean for our story from this point onwards?

I imagined planting cultivated food species that would take advantage of the nutrient-rich soils there to grow food for community. An act which would help to re-story the soil so that it may once again be hospitable to the plants that preferred fewer nutrients that once grew there. The very reason some of our previous efforts, to put the lands back to what they used to be before contact, didn't work. We would no longer fight the stories of the soil, and we would work purposefully with those truths to create the story for the future that includes different foods, traditional and agrarian. That meets the needs of community in addressing and learning about food security, teaches plant knowledge, and creates opportunities for reclamation and practising of culture. Rich opportunities for land-based learning that is not restricted to colonial notions of belongingness and an ecosystem stuck in time.

Next, I walked down the hill to one of the many thick patches of the weed Canada thistle, and asked, What's your story? Canada thistle tells a similar story to that of soil, of how the soil changed over time and became more receptive to their presence. There didn't seem to be any opposition to their presence and the bee relations seemed to like them and so they stayed and multiplied. There were so many pollinators on them you could hear the gentle buzzing. I knew that the story for Canada thistle would be one that would hopefully see their rise gently fall away. This would or could have an impact on the story of the pollinators there, and so the story for the bees would require perhaps the introduction or reintroduction of other relations they needed. Would I have thought about that before Ye'yumnuts? No. I would have thought only of Canada thistle not belonging and thus only of their demise.

The value of knowing the stories of our relations in these ecosystems is more than honouring and acknowledging them so we can continue writing their stories. Their story offers us a window into their world that reveals their own webs of relationships. A view that provides much more than a simple yes-or-no question of belongingness would yield. Ecological mistakes such as restoration failures, or re-invasion of a new species upon the eradication of another, may well have been prevented if we had been working from and toward the stories of our relations as opposed to being guided by the seemingly simple question of belongingness. That is what the bees on the Canada thistle revealed to me. To know someone's story is to really know them.

To cast judgment was to make oversimplified assumptions and perhaps harm an important relation.

I made my way over to a small grouping of young Garry oaks who by all appearances would have been swallowed up by the Himalayan blackberry and perhaps eaten by the deer had it not been for the caging placed around them. I asked them, What's your story? They told me of just how hard it was to be a young Garry oak tree. That many of them don't make it to adulthood. I replied, Well, it is a good thing that someone has tried to protect you. The young Garry oaks merely shrugged, as teenagers tend to do. They said that this attempt to help them was part of a shifting story where the humans were coming back, but what they were doing wasn't quite enough. They wanted a deeper connection with their human relations. One where the grasses and shrubs attempting to swallow them would be burned, and where some of the friends they grow best with returned alongside them. One where they could stand over and embrace the youth as they learn and grow on the lands once more. "There must be a way to write our story so that this can happen," the Garry oaks said to me.

I felt as though the Garry oaks spoke for Ye'yumnuts. That the community could write a story inspired by the past, aware of the present, and hopeful for the future—all to bring healing to this place and to us all. This narrative would be so much more than the simple list of appropriate plants that I had put together at the beginning of my journey. I'd started from a foundation of colonial, environmental saviourism that I had been taught in an education system relying only on one knowledge paradigm, when in fact we needed the language of the land healers to create a story of relational and reciprocal long-term care. To write together, to be authors of Ye'yumnuts's story and balancers of her ecosystem, would be to bring all who cared for her together. To create a story with deep ties to cultural learning, to history, to a future where children would know their stories, medicines, and foods, and would be able to find new medicines, new foods, and new relationship with the land.

I used to be an ecologist who simply brought an "end product" back to communities based on the work that I did alone on their lands (Indigenous or not). Now, I am a community gatherer, working to help bring healing beyond just the land. I am a story-listener. I am a storyteller. I am a shaper of ecosystems. I work on bringing communities together, in circle, to listen to each other. Motivated in our caring for place and each other. Uniting unsuspecting allies with shared values. Applying multidimensional land healing, or what I have come to call whole-community-level healing, as a practice for healing people and Earth. I no longer see challenges facing communities in isolation from each other; I ask instead, How can connection with land bring us together? What is missing that we need to make that connection? I look at health challenges and wonder how connection with land can be made to help. How can we create stories for land that improve the well-being of our communities? How can we create stories for land that give people of all ages purpose and meaning?

I decided I was going to bead some three-dimensional native blackberries. After going outside and looking at the ones growing on my farm, chatting with friends who were experienced beaders, and watching a few YouTube videos, I picked up my needle and thread. I knew which of the purples and greens to use, and I learned from the land and people how to bring them together. Even though I did not quite know what I was doing, I began. The thread slowly but surely telling a story. I made mistakes, had to go back and fix them, but eventually threaded together a vision similar to the one I set out with.

12.

Heal the Land, Heal Myself

IN 2022, I was called to the lands along the Fraser River in the Interior of BC because of my expertise with culturally important and invasive plants. The territory had suffered from climate-caused wildfires instigated by the devastating "heat dome" that made international news in 2021. One of these fires, the vast McKay Creek Wildfire just north of Lillooet, BC, had burned more than forty-five thousand hectares of land including four distinct biogeoclimatic zones (different land types) and ranged in its severity across a spectrum from mild to severe. One year later, it was time to figure out how to bring healing to these lands. Specifically, to check in with our plant relations, to see how they were doing.

Before I headed to the Interior, my colleague sent pictures of the area burned by fire taken in the spring, and many of the areas resembled a "moonscape." It was difficult to fathom. I could see that the soils were hydrophobic—no longer able to absorb water; instead, water would just rush down them like a river, because there was no topsoil left. It had burned along with the trees and shrubs.

These are the lands where my grandmother, Hester Sworts, grew up, and many of my cousins reside today in St'át'imc territory. Lands adjacent to our own Nlaka'pamux (Amy Tresierra) and Secwepemc (Bill Sworts) territories. I am known as one of the "coastal cousins," having grown up disconnected from my home communities on the south mainland coast of BC, so these lands were largely unfamiliar to me. It was the first time in a long time I found myself going to a place to work not knowing much about the plant ecology. I was an expert of other Peoples' plants, and I had come to terms with that in recent years. Coast Salish Elders had told me that they appreciated the help, and encouraged me to connect with their lands in any way I could. For that I am so grateful. Now I had to confront this colonization-imposed cultural gap in a new way. In a way that really made me feel as though I didn't belong where I was supposed to belong.

I had some limited knowledge of fire ecology, but admittedly, it isn't my wheelhouse. Fire suppression being so important where I live, my knowledges were largely restricted to Elders and knowledge keepers telling me about traditional land stewardship techniques, particularly the use of fire in Garry oak meadows like Ye'yumnuts and in the Tsm'syen forest gardens to sweeten land and keep the surrounding forest canopy from closing over them.

I had preliminary interactions with the communities living with the impacts of this devastating fire. I knew there was great concern about impacts to four-legged relations, in particular the winter ranges of mule deer, as well as fish relations because of the damage to riparian areas. We didn't know how the existing populations of invasive plants would respond to the differing fire severities, nor did we know what would happen to the culturally important (sometimes referred to as "native") plant species. Students in my lab were going to try to understand these dynamics to inform what would come next.

The day before I was set to leave, I felt overcome with emotion. The dissonance of being a plant knowledge holder who didn't know the plants where my family "comes from" felt . . . terrible. Embarrassing. Complicated. I was finally at a point of cultural reclamation where I felt a sense of belonging, but it was as if that had been pulled from beneath my feet. I, like many of my "coast" family members, found belonging and kinship with Indigenous communities we didn't have ancestral ties to. I knew I was going to where my cousins were, and where my great-grandmother's and great-great-grandmothers' ranches had been. I had seen countless pictures of my family on those lands, heard many stories, but I had no real connection to those lands and had barely ever stepped upon them.

The complexities of the impacts of colonialism on Indigenous Peoples are direct and indirect. The impacts are lived. Today. Here I was, living the consequences of the choices made by my family to use assimilation to protect us. Here I was, with my PhD, working in the ivory tower, in many ways living the benefits of that assimilation. This was not like any other research project for me.

The emotion I felt was also a heaviness of confronting our ecological reality. It was one thing to see photos and videos of the fires that hit Lillooet and Lytton over the past two years posted by my cousins and friends on Facebook, or to see them on the news, but quite another knowing that I would experience their aftermath in person. Once again, I was confronted with the fact that my part of the family did not live there. I could watch safely, from afar, because . . . assimilation. I could talk about climate impacts, and I had lived them on our farm on Vancouver Island during the heat dome, as some of our chickens died and our raspberries fried to the plants, but we were never in the same kind of danger; we did not endure the repeated trauma of the fires. I knew that I felt the trauma of my friends and relatives, the ancestral trauma, and the trauma of the Lytton fire to the south taking my father's final resting place, but what right did I have to any such trauma? People and our other relations who lived there lost their lives or had their lives destroyed.

Still, I had watched the fire maps with angst as they spread toward where my father rested on the banks of the Thompson River. I had so many photos of him there, smiling while fishing, the steep cliffs in the background. I realized that all the griefs I carried, personal, cultural, and ecological, were tangled together. It was a lot to face.

As we drove toward Lillooet, I was transfixed by the beauty. As we came into town, I felt immediately familiar with it. So many family stories and pictures made it so. The dryness of the air and breeze up the river brought me back to childhood memories. The steepness of the mountains made me smile as they were represented in the button design on my regalia, and I had knitted their peaks onto my sweater. It wasn't home for me, but it was part of the story of my family, and I would never be disconnected from that, no matter where I lived.

The next day we drove out to lands that had been burned by the fire, and I was filled with an anxiety that is difficult to describe. We began by looking at unburned grasslands, which reminded me so much of the Garry oak meadows belonging to my Cowichan friends. This made it feel familiar. As I discussed the challenges of these grasslands with my friend and colleague that I owe so much to for bringing me into this research project, I was surprised by the similarities in the challenges we faced with the Garry oak systems. The trees, shrubs, and plants may not be the same, but the suppression of fire, the loss of traditional stewardship practices, was having similar negative effects.

Fire severity, measured as the percentage mortality of tree biomass after a fire event, is categorized as low (less than 20 percent), moderate (20 to 70 percent), and high (more than 70 percent).[59] Due to a changing climate and a colonial history of fire suppression, the severity of forest fires is currently much higher than it should be. The first burn sites we stopped at were high-severity burns, the worst of the fire. We stood where the moonscape-like images of a high-severity burn I had been sent were taken in the spring, and marvelled that, six months later, the fire impacts to the lands appeared somewhat less . . . devastating than I expected. There were plants growing out of ash, where the soil had been burned—it was remarkable. I found myself quoting the character Ian Malcolm in *Jurassic Park*, saying out loud, "Life finds a way." I looked around and there were far more familiar plant friends than I had anticipated. Snowberry. Fireweed. Knikannik. Nodding onion. Lilies. Among them, spaced widely across the landscape, were weedy companions I knew well, like mullein, bull thistle, and lamb's quarters. I looked across the land in search of the stories the plant relations were telling us about life before, during, and after the fires. It was as if they all began talking at once. Their movements across the ashen lands told the stories of their seed banks, the animals still moving through these areas, and the power of water and wind. There were species I didn't know, but they moved on the lands in the same way. Perhaps I wasn't so out of place after all.

It wasn't until we arrived on the low- and medium-severity burn sites of the grasslands that the lands really told their stories. Once again, we stood where pictures had been taken in spring, showing barren lands, burned. Now we stood in an endless sea of golden grasses. While there were some gaps, in them we found the nodding onion, snowberry, lilies. The pines that had been encroaching on the grasslands, burned, and stopped in their tracks. It was as though the grasslands had at last been able to push back and assert their existence. The large sagebrush that was taking over had burned, with only small ones emerging in scattered places. As it should be.

When we drove into the unburned patches within the fire zone, suddenly, instead of feeling as though these were the ecological controls, or places still "whole," the trees appeared so crowded, dense, with little in their understories. This was not supposed to be the story of these lands. Or at least, not the whole story.

I am not minimizing the impacts of these fires—in many respects they were devastating. But these lands tell a story of the need for the reclamation of an Indigenous ecology that includes fire. One that stands up to the colonial legacy of Smokey the Bear. A legacy that may well have unnecessarily put people in danger. Instead of the utter devastation I expected after seeing these lands for myself, I felt tremendous hope. The stories the lands were speaking were of resilience, and of desire for human relationship. This does not mean that we do not have a lot of work to do ahead of us. There is a lot of work to do. But perhaps these fires were an expression of the truth of these lands that we can no longer erase. That the future story is one of reclaimed and revitalized Indigenous traditional stewardship practices and the food systems that go along with them. A story depicted by an image made of a mosaic of knowledges that guides our roles and relationships in the purposeful shaping of these lands once more. That we will stop trying to restore lands, but re-story them alongside the many co-authors that know them well.

As we drove home after our brief introduction to the lands of my cousins and neighbouring lands of my family, I felt such a deep sense of peace. I felt as though I was exactly where I was supposed to be. It was not long after that visit that leadership from my own Nlaka'pamux Nation sent an email, inviting me to come for a day with community to talk about the impacts of the Lytton fire on our plant relations and how we can help to heal the land moving forward. I cried when I received the email. It was as though the ancestors still found me, even though I was far from "home," and shaped my life such that I would eventually find my way back, with gifts and knowledges that could help to write a story of reclamation and resilience for the future to bring healing to these lands and my heart. A Kwakwa̱ka̱'wakw friend, Tom Sewid, said to me, "You are Umista, meaning 'the return of something precious'—enjoy, listen, and pass on what you know. You are Umista to your People, Dr. Grenz." I cried some more.

13.

Making the Old New Again:
A Call to Action from the Frogs

I learned of a story about the Bitterroot River in western Montana
through a Twitter thread posted by @BugQuestions in 2020 that really
spoke to my heart. Carving out a seventy-five-mile canyon in western
Montana, the shallow river, only three feet deep in places, is easily
crossed by humans and animals. The first white settlers arrived in
Montana in the first half of the nineteenth century, and the Salish
people, the Indigenous Peoples of the lands there, warned them not to
settle the west side of the Bitterroot River. The story goes that the settlers
ignored these warnings, and a small group of people settled that side of
the river. Soon after, many of them died of a mysterious disease.

Drawn to the area by the gold rush, the settler population quickly
grew. The mysterious disease on the west side of the Bitterroot River
made life so difficult for the growing population that in the early 1900s
the state board of health brought in Dr. Louis Wilson and Dr. William
Chowning to investigate. Tracking the illness, they created a map of the
cases and found that the disease appeared to be caught outdoors in the

springtime and that the Salish rarely got the disease. They compiled more knowledge about the disease, cataloguing symptoms—bodily soreness, fever, a rash of purple spots dotting the body, blindness, deafness, and loss of balance—but its cause eluded them.

In 1905, two more doctors, Lucien P. McCalla and H. A. Bereton, had a patient who was bitten by a tick and soon developed the characteristic symptoms. The doctors took the tick, and allowed it to bite another healthy person, and that person developed symptoms. Unfortunately, they did not publish these results until 1908.

In the meantime, a young microbiologist by the name of Howard Taylor Ricketts had set up a tent in the area to look for the cause of this perplexing disease. He visited a family whose son, William, ten years old, had become very sick. When Ricketts reached their home, he found ticks. Lots of ticks. Everyone in the family had been bitten by them.

Ricketts went on to dissect ticks and their eggs in the area, and in 1906 identified the micro-organism that causes the deadly illness. He named the bacteria after himself—Rickettsia rickettsii.

The pathogen would go on to be well studied and the disease would go by a few other names, including Black Measles. Over time, the scientific community settled on a name, first published in 1903, for the condition that the Salish had warned the settlers against nearly seventy years before: Rocky Mountain Spotted Fever.[60]

I read this story just as I was coming to the end of my PhD research that has been the cornerstone of this book, and my tweeted reply was, "Thanks for sharing. Yet another example of settlers' disregard for our knowledges and of scientists describing our knowledges in a mystical way that allows them to then take credit for another 'discovery.'" It got some likes. Clearly my sentiment resonated with others. I spent an entire day ruminating on why it was that this story spoke to me. It went beyond my usual interest as an invasive species specialist in these types of origins-of-invasion stories.

It was the familiarity of the devaluation of Indigenous knowledges that made me unable to stop thinking about it. I found myself down a rabbit hole researching the story further. I found a report from Surgeon Cobb, who was sent to the Bitterroot Valley to investigate the disease in 1902.[61] I felt disappointed that over one hundred years later, I could so strongly connect with the denigration and dismissal of Indigenous knowledge by Western science that I found in that report.

There is an established tradition of mystifying the advice and information provided by Indigenous Peoples. While it would be easy to attribute it to both the attempted erasure of our communities and the assertion of settler exceptionalism and move on, I think we have a collective responsibility (settlers and Indigenous Peoples) to dig deeper and understand how and why this happens. Mystification of our knowledges and advice has long been a strategy of those working from the Western scientific worldview. It is an easy way to devalue and ultimately disregard it. I believe from my own experiences and observations there are two distinct reasons that motivate this. The first is that in our modern world, the advice and knowledges of Indigenous Peoples may not be convenient to the goals and intentions of those receiving it. The second is that devaluation and disregard of related information makes it easier to lay claim to a "discovery," ultimately repackaging our knowledges and stealing them.

This tradition carries on today, and while things are getting better in some respects, and our knowledges are being sought in a variety of contexts, we are still merely included in processes of decision-making and research that we do not quite fit within. Our knowledges cannot be copied and pasted into colonial structures. Space must be made for the application of our world-view for the full benefit of it to be realized. I cannot help but grieve the loss of the potential of our knowledges and stories to influence the trajectory of knowledge acquisition past and present. How many of our stories could have spared lives? What solutions do we hold that remain unknown?

To synthesize my research journey, I wrote the story of the frog finding our Indigenous ecology—the coming together of an Indigenous woman and a woman of science:

I could hear the water lapping upon the shore. I felt drawn to it, but the Elders told me to pay no mind. It wasn't my time yet. There were lessons this tadpole had yet to learn from my relations in the water. In the water I learned of the Great Mystery, relationality, and reciprocity. I learned from the salmon, the herring, the rocks, and the tides. To be enveloped by the water was a constant reminder of my connection to, and potential impact upon, my relations that shared this world.

It came time for me to follow the sound of the waves breaking upon the shore. Feeling the sand beneath my new feet, I hopped toward the forest. Here I would learn the lessons of my land relations. Upon the land I learned of Western science, of the scientific method. I learned from the bears, the wolves, and the humans.

My land relations told me their world was changing. I already knew. We could taste it long ago in the water world. We tried to warn them, but they could not hear us. They were trying to fix our Earth Mother but what they knew was not enough. I could see that they needed the lessons of the water world, but they could not swim.

As a frog, it was clear to me that we needed the lessons of both realms, the water and the land, to heal our Earth Mother. It was clear to me that we frogs could not do this alone.

So I led my land relations to the shoreline. I taught them to swim as I could. I taught them the lessons of the Great Mystery, of relationality, of reciprocity, as they had taught me of Western science. I taught them of their role as the balancers of our ecosystem. To be guided by the values of all our relations, on the land and the water.

Together we learned that we need each other to heal our Earth Mother. To learn to swim and to walk so that we may cross realms for wisdom and knowledge as we need to. For the benefit of all. We called it our Indigenous ecology. And with its power, no challenge will be too great.

The frog was chosen as it symbolizes the ability to traverse two worlds, water and land. Frogs are used by shamans as they represent adaptability and are powerful givers of knowledge. I proudly wear them on my regalia. My research journey was one focused on becoming the best frog I could be.

This coming together required the journey around the medicine wheel. The journey I just invited you to come along with me on, a sacred circle. One of looking to the wisdom of our Elders and ancestors in the North. One of embracing the necessary spiritual journey in the East. One of preparing for change and rapid transformation in the South. And finally, ending up here, in the West. Empowered to work in a new way and let go of how we have always done things.

The medicine wheel teaches us that we need balance in each of the directions. Without that balance, we will not have the healing our planet so desperately needs. The medicine wheel reveals a science that has been with us since time immemorial. This is not to disregard the scientific progress of our modern world; acknowledging Indigenous science is not at odds with that. The problem is that Western science took from the medicine wheel and then carried on developing without it. In many ways, it developed in spite of it. In so doing, science has lost its balance. Are we so ruled by the fear of mysticism that we cannot embrace the spiritual and emotional aspects of science? Aspects that we have been conditioned to disregard and disdain, when there is immense value in admitting to the "whys" of what we are doing, in being inspired by dreams, in doubting our progress and sitting in the angst of that. These are all part of the scientific process, are they not? Perhaps we know enough now that we can have confidence in our abilities to ensure balance, whichever "science" you come to the medicine wheel from. The medicine wheel I present here is meant to guide journeys of land healing, but I can see that other medicine wheels can be made to improve every scientific specialty, if we are brave enough to do it. What gains are waiting for us?

Since I began this book, I have found myself in a new world of extraction of Indigenous knowledges. As the benefits of Indigenous ways of doing, knowing, and understanding are increasingly realized, their use is being incentivized by funding and government agencies. On one hand, I view this as progress—I certainly do not need to do the convincing I used to that our ways could be helpful to complex environmental challenges. However, with progress comes new challenges; challenges that we few Indigenous scholars in the sciences are trying to figure out. Questions like, Who can use Indigenous ways of doing, knowing, and understanding? To what extent can or should non-Indigenous Peoples engage with our knowledge systems? Should non-Indigenous researchers be in the space of bringing together knowledges? There are no easy answers to any of this, and I know first-hand that there are too few of us to be helping everywhere. We need our allies working in a good way.

What we don't need is our knowledges used without us, or non-Indigenous researchers claiming their areas of expertise as bringing (braiding, weaving, etc.) our knowledges together. I have an uneasiness when non-Indigenous researchers express to me their desire to work with our communities to "fix" something. I worry that my own efforts are backfiring and placing Indigenous Peoples and our knowledges in harm's way.

I invited you on this journey around the medicine wheel with me. That journey, to me, was sacred. I am grateful that you came with me, and I hope that it has stretched you in new ways. I hope that it helps to empower you to bring meaningful and effective healing to the lands and waters you care about. But like any good "young Elder" I must remind you that the lands and waters you care about most likely belong to Indigenous Peoples. It is critical that you recognize that your completion of this journey is not a free pass to take what you have learned and skip past us. There are many useful lessons here about relationality that are not inherently Indigenous, but as you take in the parts that are, you must promise me that you will commit yourselves to both the phrases "Nothing about us [Indigenous Peoples] without us [Indigenous Peoples]" and "Nothing about us [Indigenous Peoples] that isn't led by us [Indigenous Peoples]."

At the peak of wrestling with all this, to understand really what
my purpose was in writing this book and what exactly responsible
empowerment in embracing an Indigenous ecology was, I was being

*kept awake by the magnified croaking of frogs at night. It was early
spring, the time of the mating of Pacific chorus frogs where we live.
Their croaking at night sounds much like an army of frogs threatening
some kind of takeover, but still at a soothing volume where I feel grateful
that this is the sound lulling me to sleep. Not this particular year. The
sound was so loud that even with the windows closed, I could not sleep.
It was as though the frog, or frogs, were croaking through a megaphone.*

*I was out in our backyard after a few nights of this, searching for the
clamorous frog. That year, being so busy at the end of summer, we had
neglected to dismantle and put away our children's above-ground pool. It
had remained up through the winter and now sat with a few inches of
water at the bottom. I wandered over to it, bumping the bottom with the
toes of my boots and setting a vibration through the pool—only to receive
a very loud and echoing croak in response. This was it. The frog was
stuck in the pool and the croaking was being amplified by the echoing
against the walls of the pool. Cue Operation Rescue the Frog. My son
eventually caught the frog and scooped him or her out with the pool net.
High-fives all around. Mission accomplished.*

*That night I had just lain down, ready for a restful night of sleep
again, and CROAK. "Ugh!" I exclaimed. I figured we must've missed
one. The next day I got my son started on the second extraction. As he
poked and prodded around the things he had left floating in the pool all
winter, he called me over to it. "What the heck is this?" With the net,
he lifted a gelatinous mass that was stuck to the bottom of a boogie
board. "Oh my goodness! That's an egg mass! The frogs have laid eggs
in the pool!" My son put them back in the water just in time for mama
or papa frog to make an appearance sitting on top of said boogie board.
Now we didn't know what to do. Do frog eggs need their parents? I had
no idea. Forgive me, I am a plant person. We googled, decided the
answer was no, and removed the parental guardian, concerned that they*

had made a big mistake laying eggs in there and were stuck. We placed the frog on the edge of our drainage pond instead. Half an hour later, the same frog was back in the pool. Turns out they have sticky "fingers" for climbing. Feel free to laugh at me now.

We dived into learning more about the life cycle of Pacific chorus frogs and, though skeptical that this would have a positive outcome, decided to go with it and see what would happen. We watched all spring with wonder as the eggs developed, eventually hatching into tadpoles. We stopped counting at two hundred. I was feeling like a proud mama of frogs. Daily checks on our tadpoles became a family routine. Each milestone celebrated such as when they developed their rear legs. By now, it was getting warm and the water in the pool was evaporating faster than it was being refilled. We decided to add water with the hose and did not seem to lose any tadpoles. We had a local frog expert weigh in on the situation with our brood and she gave us pretty poor odds of success. If only we had bet on those odds. We sacrificed the beginning of pool season and continued in waiting, managing the water levels as needed.

Sadly, I was away working when my kids texted pictures of the little, tiny frogs. We did it! At this stage, it was decided we would move them to our tiny pond area in the front of our property, as the kids were worried that the baby frogs might not have the climbing skills of their parents yet and there was little in the pool to rest upon out of the water. My son worked to safely capture them and watched them all swim in the pond and then hop away into the bushes. They were tiny, the size of the tip of his index finger, and a video he took of one on his hand hopping away is one of my most precious treasures. I was sad I didn't get to say goodbye to them. They do visit often, climbing up the sides of the house and hopping out of the gardens as I weed. I am starting to hear them outside the window, though not through a megaphone like their parents.

The significance of this experience was not lost on me. When it happened, I had just written that story "The Frog Finds an Indigenous Ecology," and I had been doing a lot of reflecting about frogs in terms of their symbolism and spiritual significance as Elders had just chosen them for the four corners of my button blanket. They showed up as I continued to struggle with what my role was as a frog myself. As a sharer of knowledge. As someone who had learned to occupy two worlds. Here I had been, all spring long, learning to nurture a relation I knew little of. A relation that then multiplied and sprang away from a place of care to sing its song to the rest of the world.

You are the singers of songs.

I have carefully nurtured you on this journey around the medicine wheel, whether you consider yourself an ally of Indigenous Peoples or are Indigenous yourself. This was meant to meet you where you are, and to help you move toward bringing the healing our planet needs. I have shared my lessons such that I hope they have been received as gifts. Gifts that carry tremendous responsibility. That you recognize this is not a journey completed but only the beginning of repeated journeys around the medicine wheel with each project or initiative you find yourself part of in service of our Earth Mother. That the awareness you have, the knowledge you carry, will be shared through your songs to others in that service. Not so that you and they may carry on without us, but so that you may make space for us to lead you. That you make space so that we can work together in a good way. Taking up our collective responsibility to our communities and all relations as shapers of ecosystems.

It is not up to me to tell you what conclusions you should come to as we arrive at the end of this journey around the medicine wheel together. To do so would not follow the tradition of how we teach. As we part ways, it is now up to you to sit with this work, ponder it, try out parts of it, adapt the story to meet you where you are at. The very things I continue to do with it now. I leave this journey profoundly grateful that I have found the freedom to connect my head and my heart. I find myself on the other side of this journey changed forever, having found balance as a relational scientist. I leave you with this blessing:

May you find ways to make the old new again.
Through new paths of inquiry.
And alternate understanding.
May you bring healing to yourselves.
To your communities.
And to the Indigenous lands they rest upon.
Led by Indigenous Peoples.
May you share your song of the medicine wheel for the planet.
That it may be heard.
And space will be made for us.
Working together.
Taking up responsibility.
Remembering balance.
Everything is connected.
All my relations.

NOTES

Chapter 1: The Environmental Apology Tour

1 "The Scientist," iTunes, track 4 on Coldplay, *Rush of Blood to the Head*, Capitol Records, 2002.
2 Dan George (1967, July 1) *A Lament for Confederation* [Video recording and transcription] Museum of North Vancouver, https://monova.ca/chief-dan-georges -lament-for-confederation/.

Chapter 2: The Missing Puzzle Piece: The Indigenous Worldview

3 Dan George, *My Heart Soars*, reprint edition (Hancock House, 1989).
4 Jane Goodall, *Reason for Hope: A Spiritual Journey* (New York: Soko Publications, 1999).
5 Dr. Peter Cole, personal communication, July 21, 2017.
6 Sean Wilson, *Research Is Ceremony: Indigenous Research Methods* (Black Point, NS: Fernwood Publishing, 2008).
7 Wilson, *Research Is Ceremony*.
8 Eric W. Weisstein, "Brunnian Link," *MathWorld—A Wolfram Web Resource*, https://mathworld.wolfram.com/BrunnianLink.html.
9 Eric W. Weisstein, "Borommean Ring," *MathWorld—A Wolfram Web Resource*, https://mathworld.wolfram.com/BorromeanRings.html.
10 Wilson, *Research Is Ceremony*.
11 Wilson, *Research Is Ceremony*.
12 *Oxford English Dictionary*, 2nd ed. (2019), s.v. "reciprocity."

Chapter 3: Listening to the Relations of the Land

13 Chelsey Geralda Armstrong, Wal'ceckʷu Marion Dixon, and Nancy J. Turner, "Management and Traditional Production of Beaked Hazelnut (k'áp'xw-az', *Corylus cornuta*; Betulaceae) in British Columbia," *Human Ecology: An Interdisciplinary Journal* 46, no. 4 (2018): 547–59.

14 Chelsey Geralda Armstrong et al., "Historical Indigenous Land-Use Explains Plant Functional Trait Diversity," *Ecology and Society* 26, no. 2 (2021): 1.

Chapter 4: The Unravelling of Protectionism

15 Ken Thompson, *Where Do Camels Belong?* (Greystone, 2014).

16 Mark A. Davis, *Invasion Biology* (New York: Oxford University Press, 2008).

17 James Surowiecki, *The Wisdom of Crowds: Why the Many Are Smarter than the Few and How* (New York: Doubleday, 2004).

18 Surowiecki, *The Wisdom of Crowds: Why the Many Are Smarter than the Few and How.*

19 Davis, *Invasion Biology.*

20 Davis, *Invasion Biology.*

Chapter 5: It's Time for the Time of the Eagle

21 Erin L. Bohensky and Yiheyis Maru, "Indigenous Knowledge, Science, and Resilience: What Have We Learned from a Decade of International Literature on 'Integration'?," *Ecology and Society* 16, no. 4 (2011): 6.

22 Douglas Nakashima, Lyndel V. Prott, and Peter Bridgewater, "Tapping into the World's Wisdom," *UNESCO Sources* no. 125 (July–August 2000):12.

23 *Oxford Learner's Dictionaries*, s.v. "science," accessed September 5, 2019, https://www.oxfordlearnersdictionaries.com/definition/english/science.

24 Nakashima, Prott, and Bridgewater, "Tapping into the World's Wisdom," 11.

25 Eber Hampton, "Toward a Redefinition of American Indian/Alaskan Native Education," *Canadian Journal of Native Education* 20, no. 2 (1993): 1–24.

26 Sean Wilson, *Research Is Ceremony: Indigenous Research Methods* (Black Point, NS: Fernwood Publishing, 2008).

27 Robin Wall Kimmerer, *Braiding Sweetgrass: Indigenous Wisdom, Scientific Knowledge, and the Teachings of Plants* (Minneapolis, MN: Milkweed, 2015).

28 Greg Cajete, *Look to the Mountain: An Ecology of Indigenous Education* (Asheville, NC: Kivaki Press, 1994), in Kimmerer, *Braiding Sweetgrass.*

29 George Gaylord Simpson, *Principles of Animal Taxonomy* (New York: Columbia University Press, 1961).

30 Helen E. Longino, *Science as Social Knowledge: Values and Objectivity in Scientific Inquiry* (Princeton, NJ: Princeton University Press, 1990).

31 Longino, *Science as Social Knowledge.*

32 Robert P. McIntosh, "Pluralism in Ecology," *Annual Review of Ecology, Evolution, and Systematics* 18 (1987): 321–41.

33 Kimmerer, *Braiding Sweetgrass.*

34 Henry P. Huntington, Robert S. Suydam, and Daniel H. Rosenberg, "Traditional Knowledge and Satellite Tracking as Complementary Approaches to Ecological Understanding," *Environmental Conservation* 31, no. 3 (2004): 177.

35 Huntington, Suydam, and Rosenberg, 177.

36 Huntington, Suydam, and Rosenberg, 177.

Chapter 6: Bringing Ceremony to Science: Lessons in the Weeds

37 Shunryu Suzuki, *Zen Mind, Beginner's Mind: Informal Talks on Zen Meditation and Practice* (Boston: Shambhala Publications, 2011).

38 Wikipedia, s.v. "shoshin," last modified June 24, 2023, 15:43 UTC, https://en.wikipedia.org/wiki/Shoshin.

39 Louis Pasteur, December 7, 1854, letter to his friend and fellow scientist Claude Bernard, in Mark Stefik and Barbara Stefik, "The Prepared Mind versus the Beginner's Mind," *Design Management Review* 16, no. 1 (Winter 2005): 10–16.

40 Stefik and Stefik, "Prepared Mind."

41 Stefik and Stefik, "Prepared Mind."

Chapter 7: Finding Ecological Balance with the Language of the Land Healers

42 W.M. Adams, "Rationalization and Conservation: Ecology and the Management of Nature in the United Kingdom," *Transactions of the Institute of British Geographers* 22, no. 3 (1997): 277–91.

43 Adams, "Rationalization and Conservation."

44 Sally Eden and Christopher Bear, "Models of Equilibrium, Natural Agency and Environmental Change: Lay Ecologies in U.K. Recreational Angling," *Transactions of the Institute of British Geographers* 36, no. 3 (2011): 393–407.

45 Adams, "Rationalization and Conservation."

46 Adams, "Rationalization and Conservation."

47 David N. Livingstone, "The Polity of Nature: Representation, Virtue, Strategy," *Ecumene* 2, no. 4 (1995): 353–77.

48 *Canadian Oxford Dictionary*, 2nd ed. (2004), s.v. "restoration."

49 Stephanie Mills, *In Service of the Wild: Restoring and Reinhabiting Damaged Land* (Boston: Beacon, 1995).

50 *Merriam-Webster*, s.v. "healing," accessed April 2, 2019, https://www.merriam-webster.com/dictionary/healing.

51 *Merriam-Webster*, s.v. "legacy," accessed April 2, 2019, https://www.merriam-webster.com/dictionary/legacy.

Chapter 8: Forest Gardens, Webwork, and Ecological Leadership

52 N.J. Turner, L.C. Thompson, M.T. Thompson, A.Z. York, Xwi7xwa Collection, and Royal British Columbia Museum, *Thompson Ethnobotany: Knowledge and Usage of Plants by the Thompson Indians of British Columbia* (Victoria: Royal British Columbia Museum, 1990).

53 *Merriam-Webster*, s.v. "agriculture," accessed July 18, 2023, https://www.merriam-webster.com/dictionary/agriculture.

54 Chelsey Geralda Armstrong et al., "Historical Indigenous Land-Use Explains Plant Functional Trait Diversity," *Ecology and Society* 26, no. 2 (April 2021); Chelsey Geralda Armstrong, Jacob Earnshaw, and Alex C. McAlvay, "Coupled Archaeological and

Ecological Analyses Reveal Ancient Cultivation and Land Use in Nuchatlaht (Nuu-chah-nulth) Territories, Pacific Northwest," *Journal of Archaeological Science* 143 (2022); Chelsey Geralda Armstrong et al., "Historical Ecology of Forest Garden Management in Laxyuubm Ts'msyen and Beyond," *Ecosystems and People* 19, no. 1 (2023), https://doi.org/10.1080/26395916.2022.2160823.

55 Dana Lepofsky et al., "Ancient Anthropogenic Clam Gardens of the Northwest Coast Expand Clam Habitat," *Ecosystems* 24, no. 2 (2021): 248–60, https://doi.org/10.1007/s10021-020-00515-6; Keith Holmes et al., "Ancient Ecology: The Quadra Island Clam Gardens," *Fisheries* 45, no. 3 (March 2020): 151–56, https://doi.org/10.1002/fsh.10374.

Chapter 10: Ye'yumnuts, My Teacher

56 "Ye'yumnuts and the Cowichan People: A Brief History" was written using oral history shared with me by Dr. Brian Thom, Dianne Hinkley, Tracy Flemming, Genevieve Singleton, Luschiim, and Mena and Peter Williams, as well as the following sources: *Commemorating Ye'yumnuts*, accessed March 10, 2018, https://sites.google.com/view/commemorating-yeyumnuts/; *Cowichan Tribes*, "History," accessed March 10, 2018, https://www.cowichantribes.com/about-cowichan-tribes/history.

57 *Commemorating Ye'yumnuts*, ed. Brian Thom, https://www.yeyumnuts.ca.

Chapter 13: Making the Old New Again: A Call to Action from the Frogs

58 Robin Wall Kimmerer, *Braiding Sweetgrass: Indigenous Wisdom, Scientific Knowledge, and the Teachings of Plants* (Minneapolis, MN: Milkweed, 2015).

59 R.K. Hagmann, P.F. Hessburg, S.J. Prichard, N.A. Povak, P.M. Brown, P.Z. Fulé, et al, "Evidence for Widespread Changes in the Structure, Composition, and Fire Regimes of Western North American Forests," *Ecological Applications* 31, no. 8 (2021):e02431.

60 Ask an Entomologist (@BugQuestions), "When the first white settlers arrived in Montana, the native Salish people warned them to not settle the West side of the Bitterroot River. Ignoring these warnings, a small group of people . . .", Twitter post, June 8, 2020, 7:31 p.m., https://twitter.com/BugQuestions/status/1270181604623777793.

61 J.O. Cobb, "The So-Called 'Spotted Fever' of the Rocky Mountains—A New Disease in Bitter Root Valley, Mont.," *Public Health Reports (1896–1970)* 17, no. 33 (August 15, 1902): 1868–70, https://www.jstor.org/stable/41470772.

ACKNOWLEDGEMENTS

WITH A relational worldview, it is difficult to write acknowl-edgements. Where I am today, and the completion of this work, is the result of the intricate weaving together of the influence of all my relations, past and present, as well as my responsibility to the next generations. To all who have been part of my web of connections, family, friends, colleagues, lands, and waters, please accept my deeply humbling thank you.

To my ancestors of the Secwépemc and Nl'akapamux Nations, your resilience has allowed me to be here, and your influence is etched upon my DNA. I hope that this work honours you.

To my family—my husband, Joel Grenz, and my children, Alicia, Madelyn, and Joshua—none of this would have been possible without your encouragement and sacrifice. To my great-grandmother, Amy Sworts, my grandmother, Hester Robinson, and my dad, Paul McPhail—I would not be who I am, trying to make a difference for our planet and food systems, without your profound influence while you were here and from wherever you are in the spirit world.

To Cowichan Tribes, for your willingness to invite me into your community and providing me the opportunity to learn. Your land and its teachings gave me the opportunity to connect my head to my heart. The most precious gift I could ever receive. Thank you Dianne Hinkley and Tracy Fleming for your support, time, trust, and contributions. Thank you to Nancy J. Turner and Genevieve Singleton for your trust in me to facilitate the connection with Cowichan Tribes and your ongoing support and mentorship. To Luschiim, for sharing your stories, knowledge, wisdom, and challenging me to be a good listener and to think for myself. Our time together continues to be among the greatest gifts of my life.

To Thomas Sewid, for sharing stories, knowledge, wisdom, and encouragement. Our friendship is one that will stand the test of time.

To my PhD supervisor, Dr. Carol McAusland, who offered me a lifeline when I needed it most. You are an example to the academy of how to support an Indigenous student.

Finally, I wish to acknowledge the missing and murdered Indigenous women and girls. I hope to use my voice because yours was taken from you. To you, and your relations, may this work honour you. We will not be silenced.

Kukstemc.

INDEX

on relationship with colonial
society, 221
on relationship with lands, 195,
208, 215
Lyme disease, 113
Lytton (BC), 242–43, 244–45

McAusland, Carol, 106
McCalla, Lucien P., 250
McKay Creek Wildfire (BC),
242–43, 244–45
medicine (traditional), 3, 218–20
plants as, 70, 111, 113–14
medicine wheel, 13, 253–54
eastern direction, 75–121
northern direction, 15–73
southern direction, 123–89
western direction, 191–259
Mills, Stephanie, 137
mind-space creation, 109–10
Modeste, Diane, 214
mountain biking, 187–88
mutual reliance. *See* relationality

native species
as concept, 64, 140, 142
vs. invasive species, 53–54
need for humans, 69
natural (as concept), 66, 67, 143
Nlaka'pamux Nation, 1, 13, 156,
243, 248

objectivity, 91
orcas, 151
otherness, 87
Pacific chorus frogs, 255–58
parenting styles, 85–88
parks. *See* land stewards
Pasteur, Louis, 107
permission, 203–8
plantain, 112
plants

acquiring knowledge about,
54–55, 57–60, 61–62, 93, 142
after fires, 246–47
medicinal, 70, 111, 113–14
sharing knowledge about, 219–20,
224–25
stewardship of, 69
pollinators
bees as, 219, 238
decline of, 117–18
invasive species and, 53, 114,
118–20, 238
"The Prepared Mind versus the
Beginner's Mind" (Stefik and
Stefik), 107, 109–10
punum (moving), 68

racism, 26
Raines, Hattie, 24–25
reciprocity, 72–73, 174, 185, 186,
212–13, 219–20. *See also*
relationality
in Indigenous ecology, 68–69, 72,
95, 135, 178–79
in Indigenous research
methodology, 46–47, 49
learning about, 252–53
relationality, 48, 56–57, 102, 205–6
acknowledging, 165–66, 207, 255
in data analysis, 235
in ecological restoration, 210
in Indigenous ecology, 92–93,
140–41
in Indigenous worldview, 8,
32–33, 42–44, 56, 69
in language, 139, 165
language of, 133, 137–46, 165
learning about, 252, 255
visualization and, 162–63
in webwork, 162–64, 165–66, 169
research, 92–93. *See also* ecology,
Indigenous

DR. JENNIFER GRENZ (Nlaka'pamux) is assistant professor in the Department of Forest Resources Management at the University of British Columbia, jointly appointed in the Faculty of Forestry and the Faculty of Land and Food Systems. Prior to her academic career, she ran her own land healing and invasive species management company, Greener This Side, and she has worked for several environmental nonprofit organizations and charities, including Evergreen, Langley Environmental Partners Society, and the Invasive Species Council of Metro Vancouver. She is also a farmer, growing vegetables, fruit, and medicines and raising chickens for friends and family.